D0230536

Swinⅾon
BOROUGH COUNCIL

PETE COHEN

with Sarah Tay

SORT YOUR LIFE OUT!

A 21-Day Programme to Help
You Create the Life You Want

This edition first published 2009 by Rodale
an imprint of Pan Macmillan Ltd
Pan Macmillan, 20 New Wharf Road, London N1 9RR
Basingstoke and Oxford
Associated companies throughout the world
www.panmacmillan.com

ISBN 978-1-9057-44-37-4

1 3 5 7 9 8 6 4 2

A CIP catalogue record for ...

Book design by Emma Ash...
Printed and bound in Grea...

This book is intended as a ... information given here is d... your health. It is not intended as a substitute for any treatment that you may
have been prescribed by your doctor. If you suspect you have a medical problem,
we urge you to seek competent medical help.

Mention of specific companies, organizations or authorities in this book does not
imply endorsement of the publisher, nor does mention of specific companies,
organizations or authorities in the book imply that they endorse the book.
Addresses, websites and telephone numbers given in this book were correct at
the time of going to press.

Visit www.panmacmillan.com to read more about all our books and to buy them.
You will also find features, author interviews and news of any author events, and
you can sign up for e-newsletters so that you're always first to hear about our
new releases.

RODALE
LIVE YOUR WHOLE LIFE™

We inspire and enable people to improve their lives and the world around them

Acknowledgements

There are many people I would like to thank for helping me write this book. This is my eleventh book, and probably the one of which I am the most proud. This book would not have been possible without Sarah Tay, one of my best friends and an absolute rock in the writing of this book. She has an amazing ability to put my spoken words into the written form.

Thank you to my agent, Jonathan Marks, and all the crew at MTC, including Anna, Suzy, James and Kirsty.

I would also like to thank the two other members of the *Sort Your Life Out* team: Michelle Loughney and Willem Mulder. They have helped me tirelessly over the last four years, and I am so lucky to have them on my team.

There are, of course, two people without whom none of this would have been possible: my mum and dad. They are the best parents in the world and have always been there for me, through thick and thin.

I'd also like to offer special thanks to all the people who are currently on my weight loss programme, http://www. petecohen.tv. You all give me great inspiration and support.

Last but not least, thanks to Carl Benton, Conall Platts, Terry Malloy, Julia Millichope and Edward Peppitt.

Contents

Introduction

There was a man who really wanted to win the lottery, so he asked God to help him.

'Please, God,' he said. 'Please help me win the lottery. It would make a huge difference to my life.'

'OK,' said God. 'If it would really make that much difference to you, I'll help you win the lottery.'

So Saturday evening came, and the man sat in front of the television, waiting for the lottery draw. One by one, the numbers were drawn – but none of them was his. Disappointed, he decided to wait another week. On the following Saturday, the hopeful man sat in front of the television again, watching the draw. Yet again, none of his numbers came up. He decided to have words with God.

'What's going on? You said you'd help me win the lottery, but it's been two weeks now and I haven't won anything. Why aren't you helping me?'

To which God replied, 'Meet me halfway, won't you? At least buy a ticket!'

What if I told you that if you bought a lottery ticket at six o'clock every Saturday evening, from the same shop, for 21 weeks, you'd be guaranteed to win? Would you commit to doing this simple thing to get what you wanted? I bet you would. The good news is that by buying this book, you have just bought the ticket to your own personal jackpot, whether that means being more confident, finding or mending a relationship, being slim and healthy, or coping better with stress.

But if making changes was as simple as just buying a book, we'd all have done it by now, wouldn't we? The truth is that buying this book is only the first step; what you are about to learn is what you have to do to take you all the way to creating a happier life. After all, anything is possible...

While I've always known it to be true, it's clearer to me now than ever before that *everyone* can be happier, more confident and healthier, but that these things don't always land in our laps. One thing that all of us have in common, regardless of our background, culture or gender, are problems. Everybody faces challenges and has things they want to change, but have you noticed how some people deal with things more quickly and more easily than others? I've always been fascinated by this and I've spent many years searching for the reasons why.

Along the way I've helped lots of people find solutions to challenges and break free from whatever was holding them back. I've seen ordinary people, like you and me, effortlessly overcome problems that they thought they would never beat, and I've also helped world-champion sportspeople win when everything was against them. The last five years, in particular, have offered me the opportunity to learn the most valuable lessons, both through my own experiences and those of my clients. These insights have inspired me to develop the *Sort Your Life Out* programme. I know what makes some people better than others at sorting their lives out, and I'm going to share with you how to turn common sense into common practice.

What can this book do for you?

Some of you may have worked with me before or you may have met me at one of my events; but whether you know me or not, I will be your personal life coach throughout this process. You don't have to meet me or know me; as you work through *Sort Your Life Out!* I'll share with you everything that I've learned, so that you can experience amazing and lasting change.

The programme offers you lots of different perspectives on what is takes to 'Sort Your Life Out'. I will show you exercises and techniques that you can try during the programme, and which you can continue to use afterwards to help you get what you want. I will also be asking you to take on challenges, fill in questionnaires and play games, all of which will help you learn about why you do what you do, and how you can do things differently. The process that you are about to go through is not about being positive or super-motivated – it's about doing what it takes to change your life, and keeping those tasks as simple as possible. It's about breaking the habits you no longer need, and creating new, more powerful ways of thinking and acting. It's also about being kind and gentle with yourself, so please be patient and keep going.

How does *Sort Your Life Out* work?

Do you think that there are simple solutions to the everyday problems that we all face? Most people would say 'yes'. For example, if we want to lose weight, a simple solution is to eat less and exercise more. If we want to give up smoking, then we simply avoid lighting a cigarette. If we're tired, we need to get more sleep. These are all straightforward ways of changing our behaviour to achieve the results we want, and they all sound easy enough. But if they really *are* so easy, why do so many people find it hard to change? It's obviously not because the solutions are difficult; it's not because we don't have the willpower. Most of us do not have strong beliefs that prevent us from changing, either. In fact, the most common reason why people find it hard to change is simply because of the way our brains operate and, specifically, form habits.

Our brains can sometimes work in a primitive way, and one of the things they are wired to do is learn new behaviours to the point that they become automatic; in other words, we can do them without having to think. For example, if I walked up to you and stuck out my right hand, chances are you'd stick out your right hand to shake mine. How many things like this does your brain do that doesn't involve conscious thought? The answer is a lot. What springs to your mind? Driving a car, riding a bike, brushing our teeth, reading or tying our shoe-laces are all examples of behaviours that we don't want to have to think about every time we do them. We need them to be automatic so that our attention and energy can be directed to other things.

This ability to form habits can be very useful if the habits we adopt are actually those that we *want*. Unfortunately, many of us have developed habits we no longer want or need. How many things can you think of that your brain does automatically, but which you don't actually want it to do? You may have come up with answers such as, worrying unnecessarily, getting stressed, comfort eating, giving yourself a hard time, biting your nails, or drinking too much.

Our brains don't know the difference between habits that are useful and those that aren't. The easiest thing for the brain to do is to continue doing what it's always done before, and unless you train it to do otherwise, it will happily carry on with the same patterns. This is the key point of the Sort Your Life Out programme: in order to change the things in your life that you no longer want, you need to retrain your brain until it doesn't want to do the old behaviours any more, and begins to prefer the new behaviours instead. For some people, and for some habits, this reprogramming can be done relatively quickly. In most cases, however, we need to practise new behaviours patiently and consistently over a period of time for our brains to reach a point where they feel comfortable and happy.

Nelly the elephant

Did you know that when young circus elephants are first trained, they are bound by heavy metal chains that are attached to stakes in the ground? These chains are so strong that the elephants cannot break free, no matter how hard they try. After a period of trying to break loose from the chains without success, the elephants learn that it's impossible, and give up trying. Once they have reached this stage, they can be tied with a narrow chain from which they could easily break loose; however, because they believe they can't, they don't even attempt to. They have learned to behave in a limited way, and their brains have become so conditioned to the situation they do not even try to do anything different.

In a similar way to circus elephants, most of us limit ourselves through our habits, and each of us is tied to our personal stake in the ground. There is, however, a big difference between us and animals; we are conscious beings and have the ability to think and reflect. We are often aware of our limitations, but what most of us don't realize is that the chains that tie us can be broken. Often, they are just imaginary rather than physical facts and with help and support, we can break free.

The magic number

If you've ever been to the theatre, I'm sure you are aware that the performance you see is not the first run-through for those actors and actresses. They will have rehearsed every day for weeks or months. What you see is the end product. It may look like they've been playing their roles for a long time and, if the acting is really good, you might even forget you're watching a performance. The truth is, however, that they will have practised their lines many times to get them right – and to a point where they felt natural. They effectively programmed their brains to remember the lines.

To help you grow new habits and sort out your life, this book is going to focus on the number 21. Confused? Twenty-one is going to be your magic number. Why? Well, it fits nicely with a three-week period, which is a good period of time for most people to break old habits: it's also an optimum number of times to repeat and practise a new behaviour. It's rather like carving a pattern into a piece of wood – you'll need to go over that pattern a few times for it to take shape. Chances are, you have been repeating certain thoughts, feelings and actions for years so, even after 21 days, you may need more time to get used to your new habits. But more of that later. For now, I just want you to think about preparing yourself to do things 21 times, and maybe even over 21 days. The best way to do this is to be patient and give yourself time and space. Most changes don't happen overnight.

Change is the one constant thing in life. You can't resist it. Things are always changing around us and we can't stop them. *Sort Your Life Out* is about changing things at many different levels: changing the way you do things, changing how you feel and react and, ultimately, changing the quality of your life. So the more comfortable you become with the idea of changing – both your actions and your thoughts – the easier it will be to sort out your life.

 What lies behind us and what lies before us are tiny matters, compared to what lies within us.
Ralph Waldo Emerson

Set in your ways

Over the last 20 years, neuroscientists have confirmed that when we learn to do something, we form new connections in our brain that reinforce our behaviour: this is called 'plasticity'.[1] Plasticity means that the brain is not hardwired, and that new circuits can be formed to override older ones. In other words, it's not impossible or even too late to change your behaviour. As much as you may think you are 'set in your ways', and no matter how old you are or how long you've been doing something, you can change if you want to.

 We are what we repeatedly do. Excellence, then, is not an act, but a habit.
Aristotle

As they say, there's no time like the present! So let's see how quickly your brain can learn. Read through this exercise, then put down the book and actually do it! It only takes a couple of minutes, and it will help you to see how easy it can be to reprogramme your brain.

Cross your arms as you usually would. Notice which arm is on top. How does this feel? Probably quite comfortable and normal. Now uncross your arms and fold them the other way; i.e., if your right arm was on top first of all, fold your arms so the left arm is on top. Notice how this feels. Chances are, this may feel a bit strange or even quite uncomfortable. Now I want you to go back to your original position. Notice how comforting this feels – how easy it is to go back to the way you usually cross your arms. Now I want you to uncross and cross your arms 21 times – each time putting a different arm on top. Stop after 21 times and see if you can tell which arm is on top. Compare how it feels to have both the left and right arm on top, and whether it's starting to feel easier to have either arm on top.

Some people find that after doing this exercise once, they notice a big difference in how comfortable they feel: other people need to do it a few more times or for a couple of minutes every day before they start to feel at ease. Whatever your experience, I can guarantee that if you do this exercise every day, it will begin to feel normal to fold your arms either way.

This is a simple example of how your brain can learn to do something new: it just requires repetition, a willingness to experience a little discomfort in the short term and, interestingly, a sense of playfulness. You can make exercises like this fun by adopting a sense of adventure. For example, how would it feel if you slept on the other side of the bed; if you swapped your knife and fork around to different hands; or if you moved your computer mouse with your other hand? At the outset, it may definitely feel a little bit strange and uncomfortable, and you might even hear a voice in your head saying, 'This is not me. This is not how I do things.'

And this leaves you with a choice. You can define yourself by your actions if you want to, or you can choose to realize that you are more than the sum of your habits. Habits are just things that you do regularly and unconsciously, so you just need to be prepared to practise for a while until new behaviours and actions feel OK. It really is that simple.

How does your garden grow?

I recently had a fire at my home, and I lost pretty much all of my possessions. When the builders came in to rebuild the place, they tossed all the old stuff into the garden, including the bath. I don't know where the idea came from but I decided I wanted to use the bath to grow some herbs. I've always had plants in my home, but I'd never grown anything myself.

I wanted to experiment. I bought some soil and seeds, followed the instructions on the packets and waited. My mum always jokes that as a baby who was born prematurely, I was in a hurry to get into the world and sometimes it feels like I've rushed around ever since. It was an interesting experience for me to have to wait.

I didn't stand over the bath every day shouting encouragement, but I checked every now and again and watered the soil to keep it moist. Then, one day, I spotted the first bit of green. It was the top of a chive: just one tiny chive, but it was a start. Then the coriander started to come through and, soon after that, I had mint and basil as well. I watched in amazement as these beautiful herbs started to flourish. I had done the preparation and I had tended to them – and then I simply waited.

When you are going through this programme, you will need to adopt a similar approach. You need to prepare and be consistent with your practice, and you must learn to wait. When you do something over and over again – like watering a plant – you are nurturing a new behaviour. And if you remain patient, you'll find that you can grow whatever you want – whether it's the habit of eating healthily, being more confident or living your life in a happier way. Hopefully you are now starting to realize that while you may have been acting in a certain way for some time, you don't have to carry on doing this. You may be the problem, but you are also the solution. This programme works because it's about *you* taking action.

How should you work through the programme?

The first chapter of this book is called 'Sort Yourself Out', and it's important that you work through this section before going any further. 'Sort Yourself Out' is about acknowledging that you deserve to change, regardless of what's happened to you in the past. By the end of this chapter, you will have a better understanding of why your life is the way it is, and you will also have a strong emotional foundation on which to build other changes. The rest of the programme covers the four areas of life that I have found through my work to be the ones that most often cause people concern: health, weight loss and body image; self-esteem and confidence; relationships; and happiness.

We all have different things in our lives that we want to sort out, and it would be difficult to cover every scenario in this book; however, these sections will provide you with the building blocks of physical and emotional change so that you are better able to tackle specific situations on your own. For example, if you don't enjoy your job, by working on your own confidence, clarifying how you relate to others and finding out what makes you happy, you will have a clearer view of how to change your working life. Or, if you have money problems, by sorting yourself out, building your self-esteem and examining what makes you happy, you will be in a stronger position to implement specific financial advice.

You can choose to work through health, weight loss and body image, self-esteem and confidence, relationships and happiness in that order; or you can personalize your programme. After Chapter One, there is a short questionnaire that may help you to work out which areas of your life need the most attention. Whatever order you choose to work through the book, the key thing is that you are inspired, that you get results and that you have fun in the process.

Sort yourself out

Sorting yourself out is all about accepting your past and acknowledging that, whatever has happened to you previously, you *can* change – and you *deserve* to change. You will become aware of why you act the way you do in stressful situations; why you have certain habits; and why you carry around 'baggage', such as your attitudes, reactions and beliefs. When you have this awareness, you have the chance to become stronger and more balanced. This sense of balance will make it easier for you to work on your health, self-esteem, relationships and general happiness levels, and rather than achieving temporary or superficial quick fixes, you'll experience long-lasting changes.

Sort out your health, fitness and weight loss

By following this 21-day programme, you will learn how to feel good about the food you eat and the activity/exercise you do. This is not a diet, because on this programme you'll learn how to enjoy being active, how to eat what your body needs rather than what you think you want, and how to address any emotional issues that usually get in the way of being healthier. You will start to lose any excess weight you are carrying or, if you are already at the right weight for you, you will discover a way of maintaining it in a healthy and sustainable way.

Sort out your confidence and self-esteem

We all have situations that make us feel a bit nervous, but some people find that their lack of self-esteem makes them feel worthless and stops them from doing the things they want to do. This chapter is about feeling comfortable in any situation, so that you are not limited or prevented from doing anything. You will learn how to accept yourself and appreciate who you are. Confidence is a state of mind, and I will show you how to change the way you feel in quick and simple ways.

Sort out your relationships

While technology may make our lives easier in some respects, our reliance on mobile phones and computers can make us feel isolated. As humans, we need to interact with other people so that we can feel loved, supported and appreciated. This chapter will show you how to communicate better with those closest to you, whether they are your partner, children, family members, friends or colleagues. By learning how to see the world through other people's eyes, you'll discover the secret to enjoying healthy, meaningful relationships.

Sort out your happiness

The final chapter of this book is about unlocking the secrets to a happier life. It's not about chasing happiness by having more of anything in particular, but about being happy with what you already have. Although it is hard to quantify any emotion, with the help of a team of psychologists, I have developed an equation so that you can work out just how happy you are and what you need to do to become even happier.

You get back what you give out

So we're almost ready to start sorting ourselves out, but before we get started, I want to tell you a story.

A son and his father were walking in the mountains when suddenly the boy fell, hurt himself and screamed: 'AAAhhhhhhhhhh!!!'

To his surprise, he heard a voice somewhere else in the mountains: 'AAAhhhhhhhhhh!!!'

Curious about who it was, he yelled, 'Who are you?'

He received the answer: 'Who are you?'

And so he shouted back, 'I admire you!'

The other voice answered: 'I admire you!'

Angered at what he thought was a sarcastic response, the boy screamed 'Coward!'

Back came the mocking voice: 'Coward!'

The boy looked to his father and asked, 'What's going on?'

The father smiled, and said, 'My son, pay attention.'

The father then screamed: 'You are a champion!'

And the voice answered: 'You are a champion!'

The boy was surprised, but didn't understand.

So his father explained. 'People call this an echo; but really this is life. It gives you back everything you say or do. Our life is simply a reflection of our actions. If you want more love in the world, create more love in your heart. If you want your team to work harder, you have to work harder, too. This relationship applies to all aspects of life. Life will give you back everything you have given to it.'

Many years ago, I used to teach aerobics in several gyms and leisure centres. In order to get the group really working up a sweat, I had to make sure that I had ten times more energy than everybody else. I really exaggerated my moves and jumped up and down like a madman – all in the hope that the women in the class would feel motivated. If I gave 100 per cent, even the most enthusiastic women would only give 80 per cent and if I gave 80 per cent, nobody would give more than 60. I found that no matter how much energy I put into my classes, nobody was ever as motivated as I was.

You can show everyone around you how to get the most out of life by putting in as much as you can. However valid your excuses for not doing this (family, work and other commitments), you have to see overcoming these excuses and situations as part of the challenge. There are some things in life that you can't change because they are out of your control, so you need to work with them and around them – and I know you can do it. So, let me ask you a question: how much are you up for this? Will you dip your toe in the water or will you dive in? I'm always up for it, and I'm excited and ready to support you now. I'm totally committed and ready to give you 100 per cent. You've already met me halfway by buying this book, so now I challenge you to go all the way to winning your personal jackpot.

SORT YOUR LIFE OUT:
Sort Yourself Out

Desperate to meet his guru, a Buddhist follower walked for many days and climbed many mountains until, at last, he came face to face with the man who had inspired his beliefs. As soon as he arrived, the follower started talking about himself and his life, almost without stopping, until the guru interrupted him to offer him a cup of tea. Somewhat taken aback at having been interrupted, the follower accepted the offer. He then started to talk again and the guru began to pour the tea. The man talked and talked, and the guru poured and poured, until the cup started overflowing. The follower didn't notice that the tea was pouring off the table until it was dripping on his legs.

'What are you doing?' he asked, as the hot water burned his knees.

'Can you not see that you are just like the tea cup?' said the guru. 'You are so full of things that you think you need, there's no room for anything new. You will never learn anything until you make room for it.'

Many people who say they want to change something in their lives are so full of reasons why they *can't* change, or why it is too difficult, that there is hardly any space in their minds to even consider an alternative. For this reason, it's important to start the process of sorting out your life by sorting out yourself. You may be wondering what I mean by this; after all, aren't they the same thing? Well, sorting your life out involves lots of different things, depending on your personal needs. For example, some of you will want to sort out your relationships, and others will be most focused on sorting out their health. But one thing that everybody needs to do first is sort themselves out.

Sorting yourself out means learning how to put yourself first, and breaking away from the habits that may be standing in your way. Once you've done this, you can move on to work on specific areas of your life that need some attention so that you become more confident, happier, healthier and more appreciative of yourself.

In this part of the programme, we'll look at how life resembles a game, and how the way in which we play it shapes us to have certain habits and behaviours. We'll examine the fears that stop most of us from changing, and work out how to overcome them. We'll also establish the mindset that you will need to adopt to sort your life out, and get going with a little goal-setting. After working through this, you will be ready to start using the first of the *Sort Your Life Out* tools. Let's start by looking at what I mean by 'the game of life'.

The game of life

One of the things I suggest to people who really want to sort out their lives, is that they view those lives as a bit of a game. It's a bit like sorting out the game that you're playing, and making sure you play according to the rules. Looking back at the earlier part of my life, I didn't play the game very well. This was partly because I felt like I was playing according to somebody else's rules, and it took me a long time to realize what the game was all about.

The game that I think most closely resembles life, and the one I want you to think about, is Snakes and Ladders. This game was invented in India during the 16th century, and it was meant to teach children about the consequences of good and bad deeds. It was, in fact, created to mirror life. The ladders represented positive qualities, like generosity and kindness, and the snakes represented negative qualities or actions, such as murder, greed and anger. There were more snakes than ladders, to show children that it's harder to do good deeds. It's clear that this game has always tried to portray the notion that life is challenging. So how challenging do you find your life? Do you sometimes feel like you're winning or losing the game? What is the game like for you?

Snakes and Ladders

Do you sometimes feel like you're skipping up ladders and winning, and then, at other times, falling a long way down a slippery snake? When you're falling, it may seem like you don't have any control over the game. You roll the dice, and chance determines where you go next.

It may also feel like you continually go up the same

ladders and down the same snakes, experiencing the same ups and downs, over and over again. I see many people get caught up in this up-and-down pattern. For example, many people get over a painful relationship by rushing into another one because they want another ladder to climb up as soon as possible. But if the ladder leads them to a relationship with the same issues as before, they soon find themselves tumbling down another snake – and so the pattern repeats. The same cycle happens with people who shop to make themselves feel better. There's nothing like a serious retail binge to make you feel like you're climbing a ladder, but when you see your credit card bill, you can feel like you're sliding straight down to the bottom of the board. Addictions, too, usually follow the same high-low pattern: drink, drugs, food and nicotine are all ladders that lead to long, steep snakes.

Learning to play by your own rules

In this book, I want you to re-learn how to play the game of life by playing *your* way. When you learn to play this way, you will find that no matter what hurdles arise, you can turn things around – and win! You can redesign the board so that there are far more ladders than snakes, and you can begin to control all of your own moves. And when you come across snakes, in any form, you will be able to find a way to jump over them. I want you to realize that many of the snakes you come across are, in fact, illusions or challenges that you have created in your own head. What's more, many of the ladders that seem too difficult to climb are actually not as steep as you think they are. I'm going to share with you the ways in which you can deal with *everything* that life throws at you.

Before I start showing you how to change the way you play, I want to share a story with you.

Once upon a time a little baby boy popped out into the world a few weeks before he was supposed to. He came out of the womb bursting with energy. He was in a hurry to see what was on offer, and this attitude set the pace for the rest of his life. He never wanted to sit still. As far as he was concerned, the world was a massive playground and he was at the centre of it. He played his own game of Snakes and Ladders, and for a long time he seemed to spend most of his time skipping up ladders. To him, every day was a blank canvas, and a fresh start. He had no concept of yesterday or tomorrow because all he could think about was now. His days generally involved pulling things apart, shouting, screaming, hiding things, joking, running about, skipping, jumping and finding other ways of expressing himself. He was curious and wanted to explore everything around him. He didn't care what anybody else thought of him. He wasn't self-conscious. He was totally in love with himself. He simply enjoyed life and believed he could do anything – and, boy, was he certainly going to try!

For the first four years of this little boy's life, he maintained this strong spirit to create, explore and entertain. But, of course, nothing stays the same in life, and soon enough people told him to: 'Sit still', 'Be quiet', 'Do as you're told', and so on. But he didn't understand what all of this meant. He didn't understand why he was being told to do things in a different way. This was when he discovered that, in amongst the ladders, there were some slippery snakes.

His parents became embarrassed and exhausted by his

incessant energy, and they tried to keep an eye on him. At school, his teachers wanted him to sit still and listen. This was fine when he found his lessons interesting; but, more often than not, the little boy found school life boring, and would wander off and muck about. He became the class clown, and the attention he got from his teachers was negative. This was when life stopped being magical, full of fun and excitement, and started to become the serious world of grown-ups. Suddenly things weren't quite so enjoyable any more.

He heard lots of 'Do this' and 'Don't do that'; he was told not to answer back, touch things, run around or put his elbows on the table. He was told to do as he was told, do the right thing, and do his homework. It went on and on, and he started to feel confused about what was right, and what was wrong. This often made him feel unhappy and uneasy. He wanted to be the centre of his own magical world but when he realized he had to conform and follow certain rules, he started to get into trouble.

Now, of course, all of us have to grow up at some point, and we all need a certain amount of structure and guidance in our lives. But this little boy really didn't like being told what and what not to do. He didn't want to sit still, and do what other people wanted. Over and over again, he heard his parents say, 'You never think of anyone but yourself', and this was true. He didn't think of anyone apart from himself, because all he wanted to do was express himself and do what came naturally to him.

After being told off so many times, he stopped entertaining himself and became very good at thinking about everyone else. He stopped climbing ladders and thought about how his actions affected other people. As a result, he started to care about others' needs more than his own. He became self-conscious and spent a lot of time comparing himself to other people. He got very good at thinking, but he learned to suppress rather than express his feelings. Although he still had his adventurous, playful spirit, it became clouded by his insecurity and the desire to be liked and accepted by others. His cloud of insecurity and anxiety started to get bigger, and follow him around wherever he went.

He got so used to this ever-present cloud, that he no longer noticed. It was as if this cloud had become a part of him. And, so this carried on for several years, until the boy hit puberty. Parts of his body began to move, grow and change, and he felt even less in control. He spent most of his time and energy desperately trying to fit in with those around him. He'd gone from being full of life to having lots of doubts, worry, anxiety and self-consciousness. Sadly, the carefree time when life had only been full of ladders seemed like a very long time ago.

The rules of the game

No prizes for guessing who that little boy was. You will have had different life experiences, or even grown up in a different culture than I did, but you will probably see some similarities in your childhood. Chances are, you can see that you, too, were 'shaped' by the people around you and by the experiences you had – and all of those experiences added up to make you the person you are today. In many cases there are positive and negative traits that we have picked up throughout our lives. For example, when I was growing up I watched my dad lose his temper every time he pulled over in his car to let an oncoming driver get past and they did not thank him. When I passed my test and started driving I found myself automatically behaving in the same way. It's not only habits and reactions like these that can get passed on, but also reactions our parents had towards us. Some parents become embarrassed by their children: that they're making too much noise; that all they want to do is play; that they won't sit still; or that they do things that are 'naughty', and so they try to control them. Being on the receiving end of this kind of response has probably happened to all of us at some point in our lives, and our parents' reactions possibly made us self-conscious, which may go some way to explaining why some of us are the way we are.

For those of you who are parents, I'm telling you this because in sorting out your own life, you may examine the fact some of your habits are things that you have learned from your own parents. For many people, this is the first step in changing and acting differently, because they are able to have a go at doing things in a different way. As parents, you can be aware that your own habits may well be adopted by your children, and therefore keep an eye on what you are passing on.

As far as children are concerned, I'm not suggesting that they should be left to run wild. For the world to work, we all need to learn how to conduct ourselves in an acceptable manner. However, I think that there can be a balance between teaching children how to fit in with society, while also maintaining a sense of their own individuality. This requires parents to judge what is realistic for children of different ages. For example, a child of seven years old should be able to behave well through a two-hour meal in a restaurant, but no energetic toddler is likely to want to sit quietly in this situation. It's natural for toddlers to want to explore their surroundings, and, of course, if they are prevented from doing this, the only way they know how to get attention is to make noise. Some adults may look at a squealing toddler and think he or she is badly behaved; but the truth is that the environment is not appropriate for the child. And that child's parents and the adults around him have expectations that are also inappropriate. Because children of this age can't express themselves, when their parents try to control their behaviour inappropriately, they internalize their thoughts and feelings. This process often leads to insecurity.

In these kinds of situations, parents have a choice: they can either judge what environments are appropriate for their children, and the age at which they are ready to learn how to behave in different situations, or they can be flexible and prepared to adapt situations to fit the needs of each individual child. This doesn't mean pandering to children, but it is important to acknowledge that their needs change as they grow up, as does their ability to communicate and express themselves. By helping our children communicate their feelings, we make it easier for them to deal with their emotions in later life.

When the game stops being fun

It's natural for us to express ourselves, and every one of us has our own unique way of doing so. Some people like to joke, laugh and have fun. Others find that they feel most at home when they're painting or drawing. Some people express themselves by being active; and others by building and inventing things. For some people, self-expression means being with and caring for animals; and still others relax by gardening, or singing and making music. Young children are encouraged to do things like this because they're considered to be 'learning activities'. More importantly, perhaps, it is through these activities – which are, in childhood, effectively a form of play – that they get a sense of who they are.

Sadly, despite some circles of parenting theory suggesting that children should be allowed to express themselves, the reality is that many children are not allowed to nurture their self-expression, and they begin to internalize their feelings. So rather than say what they feel or express themselves in the ways in which they feel most comfortable, many children keep their feelings bottled up and they worry about what other people think of them. They aren't allowed to spend a lot of time playing because they have to go to school, do homework, be with their family and fulfil all the other obligations that get put on them. This often gives rise to negative emotions like anger, frustration and fear. This is happening at earlier ages and although lots of these obligations are a necessary part of life, they often become the main part of life.

 The reason angels can fly is that they take themselves so lightly.
G. K. Chesterton

You should grow up

As adults, we find ourselves saying things like 'I don't have time for that', 'That's silly', 'You are "too old" to do that', or even 'Grow up'. We start to train children to become adults rather than simply letting them be children. We try to squeeze them into a structured world where there are social rules and regulations (the snakes in the game of life) and they become insecure because they don't feel like they belong. It's a bit like trying to put a square peg in a round hole: young children are just not ready to fit in to the adult world. When we enter the adult world, we become fully paid-up members. It's as if we forget about the time when our world was great and everything was magical.

Even though there are some people for whom belonging is less of a need, we are social beings. Therefore, most of us want to belong to the 'right' group and we want other people to acknowledge us as being good enough. The ironic thing is that as much as we try to fit in, most of us still end up feeling that we're not good enough on at least one occasion during our lifetimes. We've all been in situations where we felt insecure, but danger lies when we carry that feeling with us for a long time. Many people practise feeling insecure over and over again until it becomes a habit. And that's when we really believe that we aren't worth anything.

The roots of 'I'm not good enough'

There are any number of things that may have played a role in creating the cloud of insecurity and anxiety that you carry around with you – your education or religious environment, perhaps, or your family upbringing, and the values and expectations your parents shared. I'm not saying that we should blame anyone for the way we are and, chances are, your parents simply did what they thought was best for you. But, if we choose to look at this from a point of interest rather than blame, it can be very helpful to acknowledge that there are reasons why you have a voice inside your head that tells you 'There is something wrong with me' or 'I am not good enough'.

Most of the people with whom I've worked have found it interesting to become aware of how their experiences have affected them because this allows them to realize one critical thing: that underneath their cloud, they all still have elements of that playful child who is open to new experiences, who loves exploring and who is comfortable making their own needs a priority. You, too, can have that sense of adventure and it's exactly this that I want you to rediscover with me in this book.

Rediscover the child in you

Are you wondering where all of this is leading? Would you like to make up your own game? And choose the way you live your life? If so, there is one thing I want you to realize: once upon a time you didn't have a cloud of insecurity. You were free, happy and comfortable with yourself. You played the game according to your own rules, found it easy to go up ladders and barely noticed that there were any snakes. You did what felt natural to you and you were allowed to do that. For many people, that's when they felt their happiest. It is only when we get older that we start to see snakes at every opportunity (even when they aren't there).

Earlier in this book I told you about how to reprogramme your behaviours through repetition. That's the practical side of sorting your life out. The other thing you have to do to ensure that your changes are long-lasting is to rediscover the part of you that is adventurous – the part that wants to try new things, that is willing to have a go, and that doesn't care about what others think. I want you to be as excited about changing as you were when you were a little kid and you found a great new game to play. I want you to be inspired about sorting out your life because that is how you will be most successful at making changes.

Let me ask you...

Let me ask you how it feels to think of life as a game of Snakes and Ladders? Some of you may not feel comfortable with this idea because it seems a bit strange. You may also have pre-conceptions that make you believe that changing is going to be really difficult – which rules out the idea that it can be fun as well! You may already be focusing on all the snakes you might potentially come across. But I'm going to let you into a secret: nearly every person I've worked with who has success-fully changed something in their lives was inspired by what they were doing. They wanted a result; they'd had enough of sliding down snakes, so they were prepared to do whatever it took to find those ladders. Even when things didn't work out exactly as planned, they didn't give up. They got pleasure out of doing things differently and learned to prefer their new behaviour to the way they operated before. They embraced the challenge because they were inspired by the thought of life becoming better.

People who aren't inspired tend to go back to their old habits because they don't enjoy the game – even when the winning streaks or ladders present themselves more regularly. Old habits feel safer and more familiar. For example, lots of people aren't *inspired* by the idea of getting slimmer and fitter. They feel like they *have to* change. They may even have had it suggested by other people. And so as they deny themselves pleasures, and grow to hate every second of their journey, the whole experience becomes negative. They aren't inspired by the process, because there is no pleasure involved. It is, therefore, no wonder that they go back to doing what they used to do before – because they associate more pleasure with their old habits, even if they were preventing them from living life to the fullest. And so, it is time to play again and see what you can do. Let's work together.

 Life is playfulness ... we need to play so that we can rediscover the magical around us.
Flora Colao

It's time to be selfish

As well as asking you to become inspired and childlike (notice, I didn't say 'childish'), I'm also going to suggest that you make *yourself* a priority. Dare I even say that I'm going to suggest you become a little bit selfish? How do you feel when you read this? What does 'selfish' mean to you? More often than not, we see selfishness as a negative trait, but let's try and look at it in a different way.

If you've ever been on a plane, do you remember what

advice you were given during the safety demonstration? Put on your own oxygen mask before you help other people, including children. For most of us, that idea goes completely against the basic premise of a caring society: that we should put other people before ourselves. But what I am suggesting is something different. I don't mean that you have to stop caring for other people, or that you become self-obsessed; I simply mean that being 'selfish' means taking care of yourself and, in that way, maintaining a healthy level of self-esteem.

Unlike many other species (except primates), humans are, from birth, totally dependent on other people for our survival. We need people – usually a parent – to feed us, keep us warm and safe, and make sure we're clean and cared for. This dependency makes it easier for us to take on the behaviours of those who care for us, because this is what we see and experience. In essence, we live what we learn. As we become older, we need to learn how to depend on ourselves, and how to do things our own way.

Many of the people I've worked with are mothers, and when I suggest that they start to do more things for themselves, they struggle to break the pattern of putting their children first. They think that by caring for their own needs, they're not doing what a mother should. But ultimately, we all want our children to become independent and feel good about themselves, and the most effective way of helping them do this is to show them how it's done.

We often say 'do as I say, not as I do', when, in reality, the most effective way to help a child achieve a sense of self-worth is to set an example, by treating yourself with respect. Not only will you be better able to look after others if you are taking good care of yourself, but other people are more likely to treat you with respect, too. There is so much to be gained out of life, but in order to enjoy it all you have to be prepared to engage with it.

Some people think that by affirming and accepting themselves – making themselves a priority – they'll be seen in a negative light or considered to be 'selfish'. However, one thing I've learned over the years, both from personal experience and through working with other people, is that we don't sort ourselves out by focusing on other people. To change things for the better, you have to focus on yourself; by doing this, you are better able to help, support and inspire others, and you will find that people enjoy spending time with you for these reasons. It might sound like a cliché, but if you treat yourself like a prize, you might inspire others to do the same thing. Unfortunately, this is sometimes easier said than done.

Fear of change

An old farmer had been ploughing around a large rock in one of his fields for years and years. He had broken quite a few ploughs by not quite missing it, and he had grown rather superstitious about the rock.

One day, after breaking yet another plough and remembering all the trouble the rock had caused him over the years, the farmer finally decided to do something about it. When he put a crowbar under the rock to remove it, he was surprised to find that not only was it only about six inches thick, but he could break it up easily with a sledgehammer. As he was carting away the pieces, he remembered all the

trouble that the rock had caused him and he had to smile: how easy it would have been to get rid of it sooner.

You may have been skirting around things in your life for a long time because you've been afraid to get close to them, and this fear may have stopped you from realizing that you can often remove these blocks altogether. It's common for us to feel uncomfortable about the idea of change, because it's also natural to want to keep things as they are. But this fear of change creates a real obstacle to sorting out our lives. So where does this fear come from?

Fear of the past and the future

How often do you find yourself worrying that the past is going to repeat itself? Or do you ever feel frightened that you *might* make a mistake, that someone *might* not like you, or that you *could* let someone down? For many of us, our fears are about dealing with things that lie in our future, or about reliving things that have happened in the past. But, the truth is that while we can have *some* control over our futures, we can never predict *exactly* what lies ahead of us. What's more, no matter how much we criticize, analyse or judge ourselves, we can never change the past. By worrying about what might be and what has been, we not only waste a lot of time and energy, but we also often prevent ourselves from moving on. We need to acknowledge that past events or feelings are just that – in the past – and they do not need to remain with us forever. One of the best things about the past is that it's over. Similarly, one of the best things about the future is that we have a choice about how to approach it.

There is a much better place on which to focus your attention: the present. A well-known saying proposes that the word 'present' has another meaning, for it is truly the best *gift* you can give to yourself. When we learn how to be present and live in every moment, we stop being frightened about things that *did* happen, that *could* happen or, most often, things that *will never* happen.

Life is constantly changing. Anything can happen and everything we do is, to some extent, a risk or a gamble. So when we learn to control our fears and reactions, and live in the present, we are better able to face the unknown. If we feel confident in ourselves and our ability to deal with change, the future can be really exciting. Choice, rather than being a burden, can feel like a privilege. Instead of fighting against something we cannot control, we can learn how to be adaptable and open to different things, thereby finding peace and happiness.

Overcoming your fears

The things that people are most commonly afraid of include failure, rejection, being abandoned and the unknown. Sometimes these fears can feel impossible to conquer: but there is a very simple explanation as to why people let these fears stop them from moving on and changing their lives for the better.

We are creatures of comfort and we formulate ways of thinking and acting that become habits – and this also applies to our fears. All of our fears and doubts are the result of thoughts and actions that we have learned at some time in the past. They started with an experience that scared us, and which then caused our brains to protect us from it happening again. Rather like we practise any other habit, you could say that we practise being afraid. In fact, many of us have practised our fears so well that we have become very skilled at being afraid. Our brain also helps us by keeping hold of these fears even when we'd be better off doing something else.

But it is possible to learn to control and overcome fears; and we can do this by understanding and knowing how to deal with them when they do affect us. When we are committed to approaching things in a different way, change is possible. The first thing we have to do is change the way we see our fears.

It's OK to be afraid

My experience of working with many top athletes and sporting champions is that many of them are frightened to admit they've got a problem or a weakness, which surfaces when they are under stress in the heat of competition. They experience what is probably the most universal fear in the Western world: the fear of exposing ourselves so that people can *see* our flaws and fears. As we grow up, we are taught to hide our fears, insecurities and imperfections; it's the 'pull up your socks', 'stiff upper lip' mentality that we see so much of in our society. This is probably one reason why so many people are frightened of public speaking – because they're afraid of not being good enough.

This fear is reflected differently in men and women. In a culture that so highly prizes strict ideals of feminine beauty, women are made to feel inadequate if they don't conform to a certain 'look'. Men, on the other hand, are pressured to be successful. They are supposed to be strong, protective and aggressive, and they are programmed to channel their fearful emotions into aggression – on the sports field, for example, or in the work environment. No matter how our fears surface, we have been taught to see them as a weakness, and it is this perception that stops us from facing and challenging them. It also prevents us from seeing that we can choose *not* to be afraid.

Fear is a choice

Although it may not always seem like it, we almost always have a choice about what we say to ourselves, what we think about, what we picture in our minds, and what we feel. It is these choices that determine whether or not we find a situation frightening. So, if you really want to change and move on from your fears, the first thing you have to be prepared to do is take responsibility for your choices. Once you do this, you will be able to free yourself to do things differently and sort your life out. You will also discover that when you have the confidence to face new situations without being afraid, you can experience a whole new level of excitement and enthusiasm for life.

A few years ago I was giving a workshop in California. I was talking to the group about breaking out of a routine and doing something different. Towards the end of the workshop I said, as a figure of speech, 'Come on ... Let's go for it! Let's do something to change our lives!'

I looked up in amazement at this guy who was jumping up and down, whooping, 'Yeah, man! Let's go! Let's do it now!'

Within a matter of seconds, three or four people in the audience had joined him and were jumping up and down, too.

In my head, I was thinking, 'Oh my god … What have I got myself in to? What do I do now?'

It was at that moment that I started to think about doing the same workshop in England: I wouldn't expect to get the same reaction. When I get to this point in one of my UK workshops, I usually see a lot of people begin to show resistance, cross their arms, and give me a look that says, 'I'm not going to change, thank you very much. I'm going to stay right here.'

Not everyone is as enthusiastic as this American audience. Some people find it difficult to believe that they can change their thoughts and feelings, almost as if they believe these things are set in stone. Some of us feel like there is nothing we can do to change our reactions to situations; but, many of our feelings, like stress, fear and anxiety, are conditioned responses, just like other habits such as nail-biting or smoking. Feelings may be less *tangible* habits, but they are habits all the same. In order to sort yourself out, you need to swap some of the emotional responses you have for lighter feelings of confidence and self-belief. You can change anything you do or feel and I'm going to show you how.

Why do people resist change?

During the Second World War, a number of Japanese troops were sent to occupy little islands in the Pacific Ocean. They were instructed to shoot at invaders or enemies of Japan. Because of their location, these garrisons had no radio contact

with the outside world and so they believed that the war was still going on long after it had ended. Some of these soldiers continued to wear their uniforms, clean their weapons and shoot at passing 'enemy' ships well into the 1970s. They had been acting on autopilot because they weren't aware that their circumstances had changed, and so their behaviour also needed to change. It was finally agreed that the gentlest way to break the news that the war was over, was to send a former sergeant in his old uniform to formally thank the men for their service.

We, too, often act as we always have done because we don't stop to reassess our circumstances. We don't realize that there are better ways to act. Just like the Japanese garrisons, we don't always have radio contact with reality!

Another reason why we are often resistant to change is because we are unconsciously good at doing things in a particular way, mainly because we are well practised at our habits. While this is an example of a positive habit rather than a negative one, the story I am about to tell you is a really clear example of how our behaviour can become very ingrained. When the basketball player Michael Jordan was asked to film a TV commercial in which he had to throw the ball but miss the basket, he couldn't do it. The film crew had to do about 20 takes before they got the shot they wanted. For so long, Michael Jordan had practised getting the ball into the net that he had become an expert at getting it right: he found it hard to miss the basket, even when he tried deliberately, because scoring successfully had become hardwired in his brain.

Some people are so good at what they do, they become masters of their habits – and this applies to those habits that are helpful, as well as those that are not. Let's say, for example, that you want to experience being truly stressed and anxious. How would you go about it? I would suggest that you find someone who is chronically stressed and anxious, and then live with him or her for at least three weeks. Every time they experienced stress or anxiety – stuck in a traffic jam, or running late, for example – you'd have to copy exactly what they did, said and felt.

And I can guarantee that through the process of copying them, you'd also become pretty good at being stressed and anxious. On the other hand, if you wanted to be relaxed and in control, you could model your behaviour on that of someone who is always this way. If you wanted to put on a lot of weight, go ahead and copy the behaviour of someone who sits on their backside all day, and eats lots of sugary, fatty snacks and meals that are big enough to feed a whole family. You'd soon put on weight. On the flipside, if you wanted to be slimmer and fitter, you would be much better off living with someone slim and fit: if you ate what they did and were as active as they were, chances are your body shape would change and your health would improve. In fact, I have seen many people who have lost weight easily and enjoyably just by changing their daily eating habits in this way. Doing something different really can be very simple.

Obstacles to change

If I were to show you a ring doughnut, would you focus on the doughnut or the hole in the middle? Some of you would see a tasty-looking doughnut, while others would see the hole in the middle. Your answer will tell you something about how you approach life. Do you look at what's missing or at what you've got?

In the *Sort Your Life Out* process, we are going to be working with what you *have* got, not what's missing. And even if you have big holes in your life, we'll find ways that you can fill them. For example, if you think you're really stuck in your ways, are you sure about that? There's no doubt that you will have changed things before – even if it was something as simple as a job, a car or even a partner. If you believe you have no willpower, I'd bet that there are lots of things that you have stuck at before. They may not all be positive, like keeping calm under stress or walking to work, but even if they're bad habits, like arguing with your mother or drinking a bottle of wine every time you feel sad, the fact you have done them over and over again proves to you that you can stick at things – you may have just fallen into the trap of sticking at things that aren't helpful to you. And, if you think you can't get excited, I'd bet there have been many things in life that have excited you. Think back to them now. Past experiences like these prove to you that you already have lots of resources to help you on your journey.

We are used to labelling our habits as 'good' or 'bad', but I want you simply to see your habits as behaviours that you have become accustomed to doing. You are more than the sum of your behaviours. Even if you are responsible for doing things that are making your life a struggle, it doesn't mean you are 'hopeless' or a 'failure'; in fact, you are an expert at making life more difficult. You can learn to 'do' any habit or feeling; you simply need to believe that you have all the resources you need. No matter what has happened to you in the past, no matter how entrenched you have become in a particular lifestyle or mindset, you can change, and you can, actually, do pretty much anything you want.

It's not my fault, it's my brain

Because your brain will practise what it's used to doing, you will need to make a conscious effort to guide your brain to do something different. Your brain isn't holding on to these habits because it thinks they're useful to you. If you can feel some resistance, it's not 'a sign' that you should stay just as you are, because your brain isn't working against you. It's just seeking validation for your behaviour and your beliefs, which it thinks is what you want! For example, if you believe you are fat, your brain will help strengthen that belief by suggesting that you overeat. If you are convinced that you're not good enough, your brain will seek to highlight every occasion that confirms this. And, if you believe you're a failure, your brain will focus on the events that prove this to you, overlooking all the other things that do, in fact, prove that you're a success.

You will have heard the adage that we are all 'creatures of habit', and we can't take the blame for that. As a species, we are still evolving, and we can expect to have imperfections. Resistance to change is the primitive part of our brains protecting us because they don't know that we *want* to change. This is not an excuse for keeping hold of negative habits, but it does help to explain why we have them.

Before we go any further, let's just accept that habits are things over which we have control. You might be tempted to blame someone else or a particular circumstance for the way that you are, but the truth is that you have a lot more control over the way you behave than you probably think. We're not always intentional in the way we adopt habits, so I don't want you to blame yourself, either; sometimes we adopt habits, both good and bad, as a result of experiences, and even as defence mechanisms. But that doesn't mean they can't be changed. Once you increase your awareness and *fully intend* to change your behaviour, anything is possible. It's up to you to convince yourself that you can do it – and that comes from repeated practice.

Now for some good news...

The good news is that any new habit gets easier and easier the more you do it, even when it can, at the outset, seem difficult to do something differently. As you will remember from the arm-crossing exercise on page 15, we can easily become used to doing things when we repeat them. So, as you're starting to make changes, you will need to override your brain's automatic response until it understands that you want to undertake a new behaviour. You will need to focus on your new habit at least 21 times, and, amazingly, your brain will do it for you, without you ever having to think about it. That's a pretty good return for some up-front investment of time and energy, don't you think? Are you prepared to put in some effort?

You can do it

Would you say you were a positive, purposeful and productive human being? Or are you someone who is caught in a rut, coasting on autopilot? I have always been fascinated by what people have the ability to achieve – particularly when the odds are stacked against them. I'm constantly amazed by the capacity we have to overcome adversity during difficult times, particularly when I see people go from believing they can't achieve anything to fulfilling incredible goals.

I was recently completely hooked on a television programme that followed the exploits of a comprehensive school choir as they prepared for an international choir competition in China. What made this choir so special was that, prior to the programme, none of the children had sung in a choir, and none had any real appreciation of classical music. However, under the expert guidance of their tutor, they were transformed to near-professional standards within the space of nine months.

What moved me the most were the personal journeys of each of the choir members. Each one had a reason to fail, a reason to quit, or a reason to comply with the norm. But, because they were challenged and prepared to push their boundaries, they were able to compete at an international level. Whether they sing again as a choir or as individuals is irrelevant; the important thing is that they now know that they can succeed at anything, if they plan, apply themselves to the task in hand and seek expert guidance and motivation when necessary.

Do you think you know how much potential you have? Do you know your limits? If you follow the example of the school choir and trust in the knowledge that anything is possible

once you apply yourself, you may find that you surprise yourself with what you can achieve.

The big goals

Did you know that when a plane flies from one destination
to another, it rarely flies in a straight line? It takes a course
that fits with weather conditions and traffic in the sky, and
on paper the route can sometimes look illogical. Regardless of
this meandering, the pilot does, of course, know where he or
she is going and the plane always gets to its destination.

We can apply this same method to any changes we decide
to make in our lives. We need to be prepared to go off course
now and again, and to be flexible; we will undoubtedly come
across obstacles on the way that mean we have to change our
plans. But to get to our destination, we have to be clear right
from the start about where we want to go.

Once we recognize that we need to improve an area of our
life, the next step is to make the goal really clear and really
exciting. When we make something seem attractive, and we
can see all the benefits of achieving it, we are much more
likely to stick to what we have to do to get there.

Some of you might already know exactly what you want
to achieve; for others, it may not be so clear. I think it's probably safe to say that the overall goal for most people reading this book is to feel happier, healthier and more confident;
however, within that broader goal, each one of you will have
particular things that you want to work on. This is why I want
you to spend some time now, clarifying things in your own
mind, by using the following questions.

- What do I want, specifically?
- When, where and with whom do I want it?
- What will be different as a result of achieving this?
- How will I know when I have got it?
- What will achieving this do for me, get for me or give me?
- How do I feel about it?
- What resources do I need to achieve it?
- What will I see, hear, feel, smell and taste once I have achieved it?
- How will I look and sound once I have achieved it?
- What will happen next, if I achieve this?

The answers you give to these questions will provide you with an idea of whether you really want what you think you do. It's easy to like the idea of something, but when it comes to the reality, that something can seem less appealing. By really imagining in detail what it may be like – to have a new job, for example, to leave your relationship or to lose three stone – you will force yourself to think about how this change will impact both on how you feel, and the rest of your life. It takes time and effort to make any significant change, so it's a good idea to be absolutely sure that you do actually want what you are setting out to achieve.

The *Sort Your Life Out* journal

As this is the first time I'm asking you to write down some thoughts, I want to introduce the *Sort Your Life Out* journal.

Throughout this programme, there will be other things for you to jot down, too, so it will be easier for you to keep them all in one place. You can use any kind of notebook to do this; however, I suggest you buy a notebook or diary especially for this programme, and it will become your very own *Sort Your Life Out* journal. If you can, take the time to choose a book that is attractive, and will encourage you to spend some time filling. For example, you may want to choose a notebook with a cover that is bright and cheerful, or one that has a picture of something that makes you smile. This journal will accompany you through each stage of the programme, so you can record which tools work best for you, and note down your progress in all areas.

At the end of each chapter, you will find a one-page template, which is a suggested example of how you may want to lay out your journal. You can also copy this format in your notebook. Because it is a template for the whole programme, you will not necessarily be filling in each section every day: it depends on which area of your life you are working on at the time.

The smaller goals

Now that you have an idea of your bigger goals in place, I will help you to achieve them by challenging you to use various tools over a period of time. These *Sort Your Life Out* tools work by helping you to put in place new behaviours, which will eventually become your new habits. So, as well as your overall goals, there are smaller goals for you to meet all the way through the programme.

Scoring a goal but losing the game

I recently worked with a man who had attended a weight loss seminar about five years ago. Since that time he had lost more than five stone, which was, of course, a major achievement. He had wanted to do this because he was getting married and he didn't want to walk down the aisle looking and feeling overweight and unfit. He had been clearly able to see himself looking great, and he had wanted this so much that he was determined to do whatever it took to achieve it. But, sadly, there are no prizes for guessing what happened after his wedding day – he put back on all the weight he had lost and then some.

In one of his sessions with me, he explained that this wasn't the first time he had yo-yoed. He'd been through this pattern twice before this occasion, so while he had proved to himself that he knew how to lose weight, he just didn't know how to keep it off. The good thing was that he didn't give up. He knew that there was a way to do it, even if he hadn't personally found it. It is the same for you as it is for everyone I work with: I don't want you to achieve a goal in the short-term only to return to your old patterns of behaviour.

A few years ago I worked with Ronnie O'Sullivan, the three-time snooker world champion. For two years I helped him to stay focused and play to the best of his ability. In that time, I challenged him to pay the ultimate price of winning, which was to forget about winning and focus on the process. Those who consistently win in life, especially in sport, realize the danger of thinking ahead, being at the finishing line in their head before they actually get there. If you want to win, you need to be in the here and now, because it's what you do now that is likely to help you win. This was hard for Ronnie, but he realized the importance of keeping his attention in the present, which was what he needed to do to get him where he wanted to go.

It's very common for athletes to get themselves into a winning position, and then lose their winning streak. The sportsmen and women who tend to stay at the top of their sport for a long time are those who enjoy all of the moments along the way, and even the long hours spent training. They don't do what they do purely to win and so, ironically, winning comes more easily to them.

While they wanted very different things, both the man who regained weight and Ronnie were challenged to forget about the end result. By focusing on the daily processes and habits that would help them achieve their goals, they were both able to stick to what they needed to do, in order to get what they wanted.

If there is one single thing that defines the difference between making short-term changes, and achieving long-lasting change, it is enjoyment. I have met countless people who set out to achieve something, whether it was to lose weight, make a lot of money, or break a habit, only to find that after 'being successful', they went back to their old way of life. So why is it not enough simply to reach a goal? Why do so many people revert to their old habits?

When I talk about goals, I like to draw a parallel with football. Don't worry; you don't have to be a football fan to understand this. When we 'score a goal' in our lives, we don't necessarily win the game. For example, your team can score five goals, but if the opposition scores six, you have lost the game. Scoring goals isn't enough to feel like you've won, nor, indeed, to win. To make it worthwhile *playing*, you have to start *enjoying* playing the game. If you score goals *and* win, that's a bonus, but you are more likely to win if you're really engaged with what you're doing. Big changes in life don't happen overnight, so one of my aims in helping you to sort your life out is to show you how to enjoy the 'doing' of it and how to get excited about all the little steps along the way.

Having goals is a good thing, because they help to keep us on track, and they also keep us excited about the end result. Alongside this, I also want you to enjoy using every one of the *Sort Your Life Out* tools on offer. By making an effort to get as much out of all the stages in this process as you can, you'll give yourself every chance of succeeding.

So where do I go from here?

Before we go any further, there are a few things I want you to take on board, understand and appreciate. By doing this, you will be able to move forward and sort your life out.

1. Accept that you have a right to change. It doesn't matter how long you've been behaving in a particular way. It might not be as easy or as quick to change something you've been doing for 30 years as it is to change something you've been doing for two, but you can *always* change, and it's important to remember that you *always* deserve to have a better life.

2. Recognize that change is possible. All of us have overcome challenges and changed things in the past. If

you've ever moved house, you'll have got used to things being different, from the way you drive home to where you keep the salt in the kitchen. Every time you've learned a new skill (like how to send a text, how to use a new machine at the gym, or how to cook a different recipe), you have proved that your brain can build new connections. Right now, you might not know exactly how you're going to change, but I want you to believe, even if it's just a small part of you, that it is possible.

- Be inspired about changing. I have a habit of getting excited about things and I want you to be as enthusiastic as I am about sorting your life out. I'm inspired about you becoming happier because I know how great you'll feel. After all, I've never known anyone regret life getting better!

- Be playful. You might think you've forgotten how to be playful, but I want this whole process to be as light as possible. There will undoubtedly be some difficult moments for some of you, but, even in the challenging times, I want you to be able to smile. Taking a new perspective can be exciting and enjoyable – so make sure you have some fun!

- Say goodbye. When you take on some new behaviours, you need to be prepared to say goodbye to old, draining emotions and bad habits that no longer serve a purpose in your life. It can come as a surprise to some people to find out how attached they are to their old behaviours;

so, in being prepared to do things differently, you will at times also need to be brave and say goodbye to what you don't need any more.

6 The number 21 is a guideline. While 21 is a key number on this programme and often refers to 21 days, you may find, as people often do, that you pick up some of the tools very quickly. You may also find that some tools take longer to crack – and that's OK, too. In some cases, you'll be undoing years of conditioned behaviour. The number 21 can also apply to the number of times you practise something, rather than 21 days. So, you may get the hang of something by undertaking a tool 21 times, and feel confident enough to move on to another tool. The key thing is that, however long it takes you, you repeat these tools until they become habits.

7 Measure your success. You may be wondering how you are going to measure your success – how well you're sorting out your life – especially as you will want to see results very quickly. I suggest you do this through thinking about how well you are using each of the tools, and how often you are using them; this programme is full of tools and, in my experience, if you use them consistently, you will get results. When you master one, you've effectively made a change. And it is the sum of all your changes that add up to sorting your life out.

8 Be patient. I'm not someone who usually likes to dwell on the negative but I'll be honest with you here. There

will be times during this process when you'll get things wrong and when things don't work perfectly the first time. This happens to me all the time. The other day I was watching my friend feeding her baby son. He kept trying to grab the spoon, so she finally gave in and let him have a go. For any of you who've ever seen a child trying to feed himself for the first time, you'll know that it's a messy process! Even though he knew what he should be doing, this baby kept missing his mouth and half of his purée ended up on his face, in his hair and on the kitchen floor. But both you and I know that neither he nor his mother will give up; he'll keep on going until he gets more and more food in his mouth, and eventually he will quite happily be able to feed himself without painting the walls. Be as patient with yourself as you would be with a little baby. Accept that sometimes you might miss your target but as long as you laugh and keep practising, you'll get to where you want to go.

9 Keep it simple. As you go through the process of sorting out your life, you will be using a number of different tools and techniques to help you create the life that you want. I will be encouraging you to do most of these at least 21 times, or over a period of 21 days. Some of these will seem quite simple, but it is often the simplest things in life that can be the most effective. I strongly suggest that, no matter what tools you use, you resist the urge to make them more difficult. Don't be judgemental. Some of the things you try may not work for you, but a lot of them will. So, let's start right now...

Sort yourself out tools

Here are the first tools of the *Sort Your Life Out* programme, each designed to do just that – sort yourself out! There are three things you will need to do over the next 21 days. These things may appear to be very simple, but I have used them with many people over the years, so I know they work. I have also learned that it's better to do a few things well than over-load your brain with lots of things that you don't have time to do properly. While it's commonly believed that women can multi-task but men can't, psychological research suggests that, regardless of our sex, it's hard for us to split our attention between more than one task.[2] Therefore, I suggest that you focus all of your attention on the three tools that will help prepare you for the rest of the programme.

You may also find that you want to carry on with some or all of these three tools after the initial 21 days that you spend on sorting yourself out, and even after you've moved on to other sections of this book. For example, many people repeat my 21-day weight-loss programme over and over again, be-cause they are having so much fun! The only thing I ask is that you enjoy playing and exploring, and that you are ex-cited about the challenges. So let's see what you can do!

Three positive things

Positive psychologists, who are scientists who study the strengths and characteristics of happy, successful people, found that people who, at the end of each day, wrote down three things that had gone well and the reasons why, felt happier over a six-month period.[3] This may seem very simplistic, but it's often the simple things in life that make a huge difference. Shifting your attention from what's wrong to what's right will help you build a body of evidence to confirm that what you already have and what you already are are good enough.

As I've already mentioned, a key part of sorting your life out is keeping a journal of your progress and experiences. I once heard someone say that if life is worth living, it's worth recording. So I will keep coming back to this journal throughout the programme, asking you to record things, just as you have already started to do. The first tool you'll record in your journal is a record of three things that go well, every single day, for the next 21 days.

But before you go any further, begin by writing down three great things that have happened to you so far today, or even yesterday. They don't have to be anything ground-breaking – it could be something as simple as enjoying a lovely cup of tea while looking out at your garden, reading your book on the train on the way to work, or spending a few extra indulgent minutes in the shower enjoying the feeling of the hot water. These simple things are magic moments, and they can make a huge difference to how you feel, and your experience of life.

You could just make a mental note of these things; however, it is much more powerful (and you're much more likely to do it) if you keep track of your positive things in your *Sort Your Life Out* journal. So take a few minutes each day, for the next 21 days, to note down three positive things that have happened. You may find that this is such an uplifting experience, you'll carry on doing it long after the 21 days are over.

The Sort Your Life Out jar

Many years ago, I created a weight-loss programme called 'Lighten Up'. One of the elements of that programme involved all of the participants purchasing a jar (which we called a 'Fat Jar') and every time they did 15 minutes of continuous activity, they put a coin in their jar. Over time, this showed them how much activity they were building up and how well they were doing. This positive technique worked beautifully, so I'd like to adapt a similar system here, to motivate you. You'll start to see how well you are doing, how many new habits you are forming, and how much your self-esteem is building.

All you need to do is get yourself a clear jar or a pot (you may even want to decorate it) and every time you do something positive for yourself, put a coin into the jar – let's say a five-pence piece. If there is one thing I've learned over the years, it is that people often fail to realize the impact of small actions. If you are feeling really wound up, you may not think it will make much difference to take time out this evening to run yourself a hot bath, light some scented candles and soak for 15 minutes. However, if you did this every evening, over time you'd experience a significant change by helping to undo the stress and strain you've been under. Over time, it would become an important part of your routine and, of course, a positive habit.

In a similar way, by using this jar, you'll start to see and appreciate how the little things we do add up to make a big difference. Throughout this programme, there will be lots of things that you will be doing to sort your life out and I suggest you use this *Sort Your Life Out* jar throughout. Whether you are working on your relationship, getting fit or building up your confidence, every time you do one of the suggested exercises or every time you use one of the *Sort Your Life Out* tools, I want you to put a coin in your jar. I want you to have a visual way of acknowledging how well you're doing and seeing the investment you are making into your life. As you add more and more coins to your jar, you will get a sense of how much you are practising the new behaviours that will become the new habits that will stay with you for life.

Be comfortable at home

When you read the phrase 'home, sweet home', what do you think of? Those of you who are familiar with *The Wizard of Oz* will remember Dorothy's struggle to return back home to Kansas City. At the end of the film, Dorothy learns that all along she had the power inside herself to go home whenever she wanted. She didn't need to look outside herself – she just needed to click her heels. I'm not asking you to click your heels, but I do want you to realize that the place where you can and should feel most at home is with yourself. You *are* your home. You carry inside you the ability to feel at home, and this tool will be really important in the process of sorting out your life. It's more simple than you can imagine.

I am sure you are aware that one of the key elements of sorting out yourself and your life is to become comfortable, calm and settled in the body and mind you live in. For many of us, the place in which we live is not always comfortable; in fact, it can sometimes be quite the opposite. The easiest and the quickest way to feel comfortable with yourself is to simply focus on the thing that keeps you alive from one moment to the next – your breathing.

THE IMPORTANCE OF BREATHING

Breathing gives us life, and it is, for this reason, one of the keys to being comfortable with ourselves. Most of us take our breath for granted, but for a few minutes I want you to focus on how you breathe. Some people find it hard to accept that something as simple as focusing on and improving their breathing can be so powerful and improve so many areas of their lives.

 Breathing is something that we do every moment of every day. If we choose to pause and take conscious breaths, we improve our health and happiness.
Tchich Nhat Hanh

Did you know that we breathe in and out around 20,000 times a day? Many of us do not breathe well, which has a direct effect on our nervous systems. Most people today tend to be quite shallow breathers, and one of the results of poor breathing is that our fight-or-flight response is activated. This is the response that our body immediately enters when we are stressed or frightened, and it puts us into a state of high alert, which can not only be draining, but can impact on our health on all levels. Under stress, our bodies cannot grow, function and repair themselves as they should. If you think that you might not be an efficient breather, there is something you can do about it.

Deep-breathing and relaxation techniques are very important and can really improve the quality of your life. Before we look at the details of what you will be doing, you may find it interesting to learn more about the theory behind the technique, so you understand why you will be using this tool.

- Your nose was designed for breathing as it filters air, something that your mouth doesn't do. When you breathe from your mouth, you send an emergency signal to your body. When people panic, they usually breathe very quickly through their mouths (panting, really), which makes it very difficult for the body to filter out toxic carbon dioxide.

- Controlling your breathing also helps you control your emotional state. When you breathe steadily and deeply, you literally feel stronger and better able to deal with upset.

- As you breathe more deeply, you provide your body with more oxygen and the more oxygen you take in, the more fat you will burn. Deeper breathing will also help you exercise more effectively, and it helps to ensure a good supply of healthy, oxygenated blood to every single cell in your body. While these health benefits are not the key point of this part of the programme, many people feel better about themselves when they are healthier and carrying less fat.

BREATHING IN ACTION

Now that you have some background, here's what you have to do next. I'm going to ask you to work through this with me, without making any pre-judgements and without being swayed by your opinions. This tool is about finding some silence in between your thoughts. By practising this, you will be able to find some calm and stillness, and feel more grounded. Let's just see what happens as you get used to focusing on your breathing...

Find a place where you can sit for a couple of minutes without being disturbed, and then close your eyes. The idea of this is to shut out any external stimuli. Now simply focus on your breath. You don't have to do anything else. Just concentrate for one minute. If your mind wanders, simply bring it back to focus on your breathing.

You may not be used to sitting without the radio or TV in the background, or without being distracted in some other way. The challenge is to feel what's going on in your body and your mind, and simply acknowledge those feelings.

Even though I'm asking you to do this for only a minute, some of you may find it uncomfortable. Persevere through this; you can definitely do it! After concentrating on your breathing for one minute today, I want you to build it up by one minute every day so that after 21 days, you will be sitting for 21 minutes. Many people I've worked with say that this tool helps them to learn to feel more relaxed and calm, and it will be interesting to see what difference this makes to the quality of your life.

Some people find it hard to accept that something so simple can be so powerful and they resist doing it. They can't believe it will make any difference; but all I ask is that you give it a go, and then make your judgement. Surely it's worth a try – after all, what's the worst that could happen?

What happens next?

After reading this section, most of you will realize the importance of spending some time – ideally 21 days – working through these tools and sorting yourself out before you move on. Some of you, however, may want to read the remaining chapters, and that's perfectly fine, as long as you continue working on these tools. There is no right or wrong in this programme; we're looking for what works best for you.

The remainder of the programme is split into the following sections: health, fitness and weight loss; confidence and self-esteem; relationships; and happiness. There are different ways in which you can work through these. You can go through them in order, you can work out for yourself which area you need to start with, or you can fill in the following questionnaire, which will give you some feedback on where you need to prioritize your attention.

The Sort Your Life Out questionnaire has been developed especially for this programme by me and Conall Platts, an occupational psychologist. By working through the questions, you will come up with a score for each of the four areas on which we focus in this book. Depending upon what those scores are, you can see which area needs your attention the most. So, for example, if you score only 10 for your relationships, and much higher in the other areas of your life, you will know where you have to begin!

You can complete this questionnaire now, or fill it out on-line at http://www.sortyourlifeout.com/book – just click on the icon 'SYLO questionnaire'. Once you've got your score, you'll have a clear idea of which area or areas of your life are a priority for you to work on. Once you know this, you can then begin the process of becoming more aware of your behaviour.

The maximum score you can get for each of the four areas is 25, so your total *Sort Your Life Out* score is out of 100. This is a great benchmark against which you can measure your progress as you work through this book. If you come back to the questionnaire at the end of the programme, you'll clearly see how well you've done.

Please read each statement carefully and, using the rating scale, indicate the extent to which you agree or disagree with each one, by circling the appropriate number. Then, for each section, add up your total points and write this in the box on the right hand side. Total these (marked 'Sub-total'). This is your SYLO Total.

Section 1:
My Confidence & Self-Esteem

	Strongly disagree	Disagree	Mixed feelings	Agree	Strongly agree
I feel in control of my life	1	2	3	4	5
Most of the time I feel good about myself; I feel confident and resourceful	1	2	3	4	5
Mostly I feel positive and optimistic about my future; my prospects are good	1	2	3	4	5
I am in control of my emotions	1	2	3	4	5
It is very rare for me to lack self-confidence or feel really nervous	1	2	3	4	5

MYSELF SUB-TOTAL

Section 2: My Health, Fitness and Weight

I feel fit, energetic and healthy most of the time

| | 1 | 2 | 3 | 4 | 5 |

I feel in control of my diet, my weight and my fitness

| | 1 | 2 | 3 | 4 | 5 |

I have good eating habits; I have a balanced diet, I stop eating before I feel full, I avoid crappy food and I eat slowly

| | 1 | 2 | 3 | 4 | 5 |

I exercise regularly; at least three times a week I exercise for a sustained 30 minutes

| | 1 | 2 | 3 | 4 | 5 |

I am at my ideal weight

| | 1 | 2 | 3 | 4 | 5 |

HEALTH SUB-TOTAL

Section 3: My Relationships

I have just the right number of close personal friendships

| | 1 | 2 | 3 | 4 | 5 |

I regularly get to spend quality time with those I really care about

| | 1 | 2 | 3 | 4 | 5 |

I have an ideal level of intimacy and openness in the relationships which matter to me

| | 1 | 2 | 3 | 4 | 5 |

I feel supported, respected and appreciated by my friends

| | 1 | 2 | 3 | 4 | 5 |

It is very rare for me to feel alone

| | 1 | 2 | 3 | 4 | 5 |

RELATIONSHIPS SUB-TOTAL

Section 4: My Happiness & Fulfilment

	1	2	3	4	5
I am very content with everything that I have in my life right now	1	2	3	4	5
I sleep easy most nights feeling happy with my current circumstances	1	2	3	4	5
I regularly laugh, joke and see the lighter side of things; I have fun	1	2	3	4	5
I tend to focus on what I have got/achieved rather than dwelling on what's missing	1	2	3	4	5
Most of the time I feel happy; I am optimistic, positive and lively	1	2	3	4	5

FULFILMENT SUB-TOTAL

SUB-TOTAL

X4

SYLO TOTAL

Sort Your Life Out journal

DAY:

TOOLS I'M USING TODAY:

*

*

*

*

*

THOUGHTS, FEELINGS AND OBSERVATIONS:

*

*

*

*

*

3 POSITIVE THINGS THAT HAPPENED TODAY:

*

*

*

ANY OTHER NOTES E.G. FOOD/ACTIVITY DIARY:

SORT YOUR LIFE OUT:
Health, Fitness and Weight Loss

Our health always seems much more valuable after we lose it.
Cindy Gilmore

When I was at school, my biology teacher once explained what happens when you put a frog in boiling water. I remember wondering why he was telling us this, but now, from a behavioural perspective, I can see the point! In the same way that you or I would leap out of a bath of boiling water, the frog will jump straight out of the water, and he won't go near it again, because he's learned how hot and uncomfortable it is. This is, of course, understandable, but it does pose a question: how do you get a frog to stay in boiling water, assuming you have a good reason for doing so? Well,

you put the frog in water that is a comfortable temperature and then gradually heat it up. The frog gets used to the rising temperature, and stays there even when the water is at boiling point. Unfortunately, the frog doesn't realize how much danger he's in because he's got so used to it and so, rather sadly, dies.

Inch by inch

Just as I was bemused by this story when I was a child, you may be wondering why I'm telling you this. The truth is that my work with hundreds of people across the years has showed me that there is a similar pattern in the way that people look after their health. People collect a few unhealthy habits, none of which seems that bad in isolation, but which, over time, add up to something really painful. Just as the frog doesn't realize that the temperature of the water is becoming dangerous, many people fail to realize how much their health is deteriorating, how they don't have as much energy as they used to, and how many little aches and pains they now experience. Things become worse, inch by inch and pound by pound. Each notch on the belt is bearable and each tiny increase in cholesterol isn't so bad; it's only when these things have been getting worse for a while that people reach a point when they take note of how bad they feel.

For example, someone may start by putting on a bit of weight, perhaps through comfort eating. Then their excess weight makes it harder for them to breathe; this is followed by high blood pressure; and they then end up with Type 2 diabetes. At each stage, it's 'one more thing to cope with', 'a bit of bad news', or, simply, 'bad luck'; however, because it's occurred gradually, rather like heating up the water one degree at a time, this person may be surprised to find themselves in boiling water! If they had suddenly gone from fine to poor health overnight, they would have noticed the change; but because their health problems have built up over time, they don't realize how far they are from enjoying perfect health. This is the sad reality of what inspires most people finally to change – ill health and pain.

The good news is, however, that even when you're sitting in boiling water, many health problems can be reversed simply by changing your behaviour. This part of the *Sort Your Life Out* programme will show you how to do that. By working through this chapter, you will have more vitality, and find yourself becoming slimmer, fitter and healthier.

Let's cut to the chase

What is this all about? Well, I have been working in the areas of weight loss, fitness and health for many years, and helped thousands of people to achieve their goals. With this experience, I have refined the process into a 21-day programme so that it's simple and easy for you to follow. I'll show you how to reprogramme your mind to learn the skills necessary to become and stay healthy, fit and slim forever.

The way that this programme is designed is what sets it apart from other health and weight-loss books. Most other programmes give advice, but don't focus on what I have learned to be the most important thing – how to turn that advice into long-term habits. What you will be doing here is committing to and keeping track of your practice and progress, until you have adopted these tools as automatic habits that, in turn, become a new way of life.

There are nine tools that you can use, and you can choose the ones that you think will make the most difference for you. These points are simply common sense, so there is nothing unusual or new to learn here. But even though they may seem simple, they are not, for most people, common practice. What I am going to show you now is *how* to make them not only common practice, but new, positive habits.

My experiences with the people who have followed – or are following – my online weight-loss programme, on which this chapter is based, have taught me that most of us work best by focusing on one, two or three of the tools, until they are mastered. If necessary, or you wish, you can then move on to other tools, to create new habits here, too. The secret is not to move on until you feel confident that you have truly mastered each tool, so that it has become ingrained in your life – and your mind – as a habit. You may still be working on some of the tools from Chapter One, but after 21 days of practice, these will require a lot less of your time.

In this chapter, I'll prove to you that it's often the simplest things that can make the biggest difference, as long you are prepared to make them part of your life. You can see this process like a game – a game where the goal is to become skilful at being fit and healthy. Even if you've played the game before and lost, I ask you to stay open-minded and optimistic, because it's when you're in this state that you are most likely to enjoy what you're doing and get the best results.

(Note: If your primary focus is weight loss, and you'd like to fill in a questionnaire that will send you back a detailed report to help you focus on the areas that will make most difference to you, go to http://www.sortyourlifeout.com/book and click on 'Free weight-loss survey' and start filling in the questions. This will take you about two minutes and it's really worth doing.)

Why do we find it difficult to be fit, slim and healthy?

Before we get into the detail of the nine health, fitness and weight-loss tools, I want to share with you some of the reasons why you may have found it hard to make these changes in the past, and explain how you can become motivated to sort out this area of your life once and for all.

One of the main reasons why people struggle to adopt a healthy lifestyle is because they believe it's hard work, difficult or painful – or that they'll have to give up lots of things they enjoy. This is usually the result of previous experience, when they've played and lost the game, and are therefore no longer interested in taking part. Many people think that 'being healthy' means having no more chocolate, alcohol, crisps or late-night bacon butties, as well as having to get stuck into a punishing exercise routine. But it doesn't have to be like that. Most people who successfully change their eating habits do so because they learn how to create a balance, which is what this programme will teach you.

Many people also fail to *stay* fit and healthy because they go from one extreme to another: from being unhealthy and inactive to exercising every day and eating a very strict diet. Like the frog that gets put in boiling water and jumps straight out, most people who start an extreme health programme find that they react negatively to the sudden change. When people deny themselves in an excessive way, they usually reach a point where they can't take any more, swing to the other extreme, and end up back at square one – unfit, unhealthy and overweight.

Let's say, for example, that you've never run before. You hear that it's a great way to lose weight, so you immediately decide to run every day for half an hour. You also hear that if you only eat raw food, you'll feel amazing and the pounds will melt away. You stick to your regime for a week, but by the end of this period, your body is exhausted, you can't bear the sight of another carrot stick, and you're bored out of your mind. Why? Because you're not doing things that make you feel good, your experience 'teaches' you that being healthy and fit is painful and boring, and therefore you make increasingly less effort each time you try. Before you know it, you've adopted the 'healthy is boring' mindset, and you never want to try again.

Another pattern I often see occurs when people very nearly reach their goal, at which point they give up. This can occur for several reasons. For example, many dieters have a target weight they want to achieve, but, as they approach it, they lose momentum (usually because they haven't enjoyed the process), and return to their old habits. Other people become fitter by training for an event, like a marathon, making lots of effort for a few months, and then literally giving up and reverting to their previous lifestyle as soon as they've achieved their goal. And some people may give up when they are *almost* at their goal because they are afraid of actually achieving it.

This happens because people can be scared of the unknown, and that includes achieving something different.

Many of us have practised eating unhealthily and being inactive so well that even when we go on a diet or change our routine, we soon return to our old habits. My goal is to help you to stop going round and round in circles, following the same patterns that have never worked for you. If you continue to do things in the same way that you always have, your past will *always* equal your future, and you'll end up back where you started. Even if you feel that you can't *change*, it's worth considering the fact that you can *behave* differently – and it's the process of reprogramming through repeated practise that will get you where you want to be. You simply need to do different things to experience different results.

What's in it for you?

So, why on earth would you want to be slimmer, fitter and healthier? What's wrong with the way you are now? What will be your pay-off? It's absolutely essential that you become motivated and focused, so I want you to take a moment to think about what is in it for you.

Get out your *Sort Your Life Out* journal and jot down the answers to the following two questions. Try to be as specific as you can, and write as much detail as possible.

- What would you get out of being healthier, fitter and slimmer?
- How would your life be different if you did so?

Write down how your changes would affect not only your

life, but the lives of those around you. Maybe you would have more energy to run around with your children? You would have more chance of seeing your grandchildren grow up, or perhaps you'd be better able to face the demands of your job? Perhaps you'd just have more energy to enjoy spare time with your partner? As you're writing this, think about using language that is as positive and motivating as you can. Try to use words that make you excited about changing and when you've written something, read back over it and notice how you feel. If you don't feel motivated, don't be afraid to change what you've written until you feel happy with it, and, most importantly, inspired!

Remember that there will be certain things you can't change: for example, if you are nearly 50 years old, you can't become 21 again; or if you are 5 feet tall, you will never be a towering 6 feet tall. However, within these realistic confines, go to town on what you can achieve. Challenge yourself to be as vital and fit as you can.

The aim of this exercise is to make the idea of being fitter and healthier as compelling as possible. In my experience, many diet and fitness programmes focus on how people want to look; but I believe that in order to be truly motivated, we need to think not only about how we look, which can make us feel better, but also about the impact our health has on all areas of our life. I suggest you keep referring back to these notes in your journal so that you remind yourself why you're doing this. If you are reading this book, I'm guessing you want to change more now than you have for a long time. So use that momentum as motivation to find all the reasons why change would be fantastic, and then use that to keep you going.

Now that you've started thinking about what health means to you, let's look at the key areas you are going to be working on.

The key principles: health, fitness and weight loss

The nine tools that you will come across later in this section form the foundation of this health programme; however, before we get to those, I'm going to clarify the overall reasoning behind the nine tools. That is, to trust your gut and listen to your body, and to respect your body's need to move.

Trust your gut

We are alive because of what we put in our guts – and we do, quite literally, become what we eat. We all have choices. We can put food in our guts that keeps us alive, or we can make some changes and choose very nutritious food that doesn't just keep us alive, but makes our bodies thrive. Our digestive system is quite amazing. As soon as food hits our mouths, it starts working to break down what we eat and, through many complex processes, uses it to provide fuel for every single body function, and to build and repair. Given the nature of the food some of us eat, it's surprising that our bodies carry on working at all.

Even though you may not be aware of it, your body has a clever way of knowing what it is it needs to grow and recover. You can override this system, which is what most people do, by falling into a habit of choosing junk and processed foods because they are convenient, but this makes your body's job much more difficult. However, it's much better to listen to what your body is telling you, so that you learn to eat nutritious foods, rather than the unhealthy foods you might crave. The tools in this chapter will help you reach that goal.

To sort your life out, you need to take responsibility for what you eat. It's not about going to extremes, and eating only super-healthy food; it's about eating more of what you *need* and less of what you *want*, and then becoming aware of what happens in your gut when you eat certain foods.

The tools that will help you learn to trust your gut are:

1. Eat slowly
2. Eat only when you're hungry
3. Use the relaxation and transformation tool (available for free at http://www.sortyourlifeout.com/book)
4. Avoid sugar and stimulants
5. Eat natural food
6. Drink water

By adopting these tools for 21 days, you will retrain both your body and mind to get used to a new way of eating.

Respect your body's need to move

 Movement is a medicine for creating change in a person's physical, emotional and mental states.
Carol Welch

The other overriding principle of this programme is the simple premise that one of our body's most important functions – something that they are designed to do – is to move! We have joints, muscles and tendons, and they are there for a reason! However, they only work properly, and at optimum level, when we use them regularly, and in a safe way. When we were young, most of us burned off the calories from our food because we moved so much; however, as we grow older, most of us become more sedentary. We live in a box, drive around in a box, work in front of a box and watch a box – and we don't step outside this box because we find it unpleasant.

Most people don't move because they don't enjoy moving: they think it's painful, time-consuming and boring. But if you can reach the point where you enjoy being active, you will experience many benefits – particularly if you want to lose weight. As you probably know, undertaking sustained cardiovascular exercise, such as walking, cycling, running and swimming, raises your metabolism and burns more fat, and continues to do so for a long time after exercising. It also gives you more energy, helps you maintain flexibility and bone density, decreases your risk of disease, such as heart disease and cancer, and helps to lift your mood.

So alongside the tools for learning to trust your gut, are the tools that will encourage you to focus on moving your body, which completes the nine essential tools you'll need to achieve your goal:

7 Walk for 30 minutes a day
8 Do two to three activity sessions a week
9 Be as active as you can

Sound daunting, or perhaps a little boring? Read on; you will see that, no matter what your lifestyle, there will be something that suits you.

The first challenge: *the Sort Your Life Out* journal

Your first challenge involves using your *Sort Your Life Out* journal to keep a record of the entire time you work on the tools in this chapter, noting down all of the activity and exercise you do, as well as everything you eat and drink. At the end of this chapter is a one-page template that you may want to use for your journal. You can also design your own. The key things you need to note down in this section are:

Time	What you eat/drink	Exercise/activity

Consider this a secret mission, during which you need to gather as much information as possible. The purpose of this mission is to help you recognize the unhealthy patterns that are preventing you from having more energy, becoming fitter, sleeping better, thinking more clearly, and reaching and maintaining a healthy weight, and to assess which tools work best for you.

You may already be very aware of your habits, and may know straightaway which tools are going to be the most useful to you; alternatively, you may want to start off with tools that will come easily to you (for example, things that you've done successfully in the past). If you're feeling brave, you may want to challenge yourself with tools that will be more difficult for you. However, no matter which tools you choose to start with, you do need some level of self-awareness, and your journal will help you achieve this.

Before you get stuck in, I would ask that you take your

time and reserve your judgement as you read. There is a lot of information here and, rather like taking time to digest as you eat, I would suggest you take your time reading through the nine tools, digesting them slowly as you go. Getting them right will determine how much success you have on the *Sort Your Life Out* programme.

Health, fitness and weight loss tools

Nine tools sounds like a lot, but before you start feeling over-whelmed, I want to make it clear that you don't have to begin with them all. I suggest you choose between one and three tools to begin with. When we're given too much to do, we start to become less effective. Some people think that the more things they do, the quicker they will see results; however, I would prefer that you do fewer things and really focus so that you do them well. I also want you to do them consistently, so that they become habitual. There is a lot of information here, so please go easy on yourself and take as long as you need to absorb it.

Once each tool becomes ingrained, you can move on to an-other. This may take longer than a one-week 'quick-fix diet', but it's worth making the effort now in return for having a new way of life that will keep you slim, fit and healthy forever. Because each of us is different, there is no way to be sure exactly how long it will take you to see a significant change; however, the 21 days that are set aside for this section of the programme tend to be a long-enough period for most people to build some great new habits and get rid of some old un-healthy ones.

Eat slowly

Let me start by asking you a few questions:

- Do you gulp down your food?
- Do you eat on the run?
- When you eat with other people, are you one of the first to finish?
- Do you eat when you're doing other things, such as watching TV, reading or working at a keyboard?
- Do you suffer from indigestion?

We live in a world where things happen quickly, and for most of us, that includes eating. We have more food available than ever before; it's quick to buy, and it often doesn't need much preparation. Rip open the packet, pop it in the microwave and you're ready to go.

When we eat too fast, we tend not to chew our food properly, and we also tend to overeat because we don't take the time to listen to the signals from our body that tell us when we are full. We rush headlong into clearing our plates or into having second helpings, when we often don't need them. And when we eat food that our body doesn't need, it gets stored as fat.

But there is a mechanism in the body that tells you when you've had enough. There are sensory nerves in your stomach whose job it is to advise the brain that we've reached 'full'. It takes about 20 minutes for these nerves to communicate with your brain, which is one reason why it's important to eat slowly. So slow down and practise listening to these messages, to re-learn what it feels like to know you've eaten enough.

There are four key things you can do that will help you get into the routine of eating slowly. Every time you eat a meal using at least one of these techniques, you can add a coin to your *Sort Your Life Out* jar, to see the progress you're making.

- Put down your knife, fork or spoon in between bites; or, if you're eating food with your fingers, never take another bite until you've completely swallowed the previous mouthful.
- Chew your food properly. This means chewing each mouthful at least 21 times, which will take about 20 to 30 seconds.
- Separate eating from other activities. If you are eating while doing other things, it's difficult to notice how much you're eating or how quickly you're eating it. By sitting down at a table and focusing on your meal or snack, you will be able to practise concentrating on what you are eating, and on slowing down.
- Aim to be the last person at the table to finish.

Apart from regulating your weight and helping you absorb nutrients, there are other potential benefits of eating slowly. You may feel more relaxed, and mealtimes may become a welcome chance to take time out from your busy day. In addition, eating can be a sensual experience, so why don't you also see how much pleasure you can get from eating slowly.

Remember that you are *experimenting* with how much your body needs to eat; so, if you do end up eating too much from time to time, don't give yourself a hard time. Just learn from how you feel and remember to eat less next time.

QUICK CHECK

- How quickly do you eat now? (10 is very quickly and 1 is v-e-r-y s-l-o-w-l-y)
- How important is this tool for you? (10 is critical – 1 is not important at all)

As with all of the quick checks in this book, you may want to jot down this score in your journal. Because everybody scores differently, it's hard for me to say that a certain score makes this tool critical for you: this is something you can judge for yourself by being honest about your current habits. When you have all of the scores for the nine tools in this chapter and how critical they are for you, you will be able to make a choice about which ones to use first.

Eat only when you are hungry

Although our bodies only need food when we are physically hungry, most of us regularly eat for reasons other than physical hunger. Do you know what happens if you eat when you're not physically hungry? Whether it's a tuna salad or a cream cake, the body turns unrequired food into fat. To get a sense of how often you eat when you're not hungry, read down the lists of trigger emotions and situations that make many people eat too much and see how many apply to you.

This will give you an idea of how much you eat when you're not hungry but more out of habit or because you are in a situation that triggers you to eat.

Emotions	Situations
Bored	At the cinema/theatre
Tired	At celebrations/parties
Depressed	During coffee breaks
Stressed	Journey to/from work
Lonely	Children's mealtimes
Happy	In the car
Excited	In front of the TV
Nervous	Weekends
Afraid	Holidays
Sad	Family events

While I wouldn't suggest that you don't eat at celebrations and other social occasions, you can learn to time your eating so that you at least turn up to these kinds of events with a proper level of hunger so that it is healthy for your body to eat. As for the other daily routine situations, such as eating in front of the television, you can use this hunger-rating tool to limit the food you eat during these times.

This tool involves measuring your hunger on a scale. The 'hunger scale' is an incredibly simple, intuitive and effective way of helping you to change your behaviour so that you only eat when your body needs food. By using this, you will notice that your relationship with food will improve dramatically; you will start to feel in control of your body and what it needs.

Whenever you think you want to eat (maybe because it's your usual lunchtime or colleague offers you a biscuit), ask yourself: 'On a scale of 1 to 10, how hungry am I?'

1 Not hungry at all

2

3

4

5

6 Fairly hungry

7

8 True physical hunger (your body needs food)

9

10 Starving

WORKING OUT THE RESULTS

If you register 5 or below: You aren't hungry, but your brain has suggested food to you for another reason. Look at some of the most common reasons why you might feel like eating when you're not hungry as listed above.

If you feel 6, 7 or 8 on the scale: You are feeling true physical hunger. You may have a rumbling stomach, find yourself losing concentration, and begin thinking about specific foods you want to eat. *This is the time to eat!*

If you get to 9 or 10: You are probably over-hungry, so you might overeat. At this point, it's really important to remember to eat slowly and watch for the signs that you have had enough.

Sadly, most people have forgotten to eat only when they're physically hungry, and some eating regimes and diets even encourage us to ignore hunger. Some even go so far as to tell us what, when and how much to eat – for example, 'eat two ounces of porridge oats for breakfast at 9am' – and they don't consider that those amounts of food may not be right for everybody. So it's not surprising that many of us have lost touch with our bodies' needs, and have lost the knack of interpreting their messages. Many diets take control of our bodies for us, but I believe we can be in control of our own bodies. I want to help you re-learn what's right for you so that, whether you are gaining, losing or maintaining your weight, you can do it naturally and easily.

COMMON SIGNS OF HUNGER

If you are very out of touch with your natural hunger signals, it's useful to be aware of some of the common signs of hunger:

- Smelling or tasting a food when it's not there
- A sense of knowing exactly what you need to eat
- Empty feelings in your stomach
- Mild pangs in your stomach
- Rumbling tummy
- Low energy
- Irritability
- Light-headedness
- Light nausea, with a feeling you need to eat
- Lack of concentration

HUNGRY OR HANKERING?

Other than hunger, there are many reasons why you may eat (see page 88). By now you are probably aware of some of those cues, and are watching out for them. If you suspect you're not truly hungry, wait for 20 minutes to see if the hunger is real physical hunger or a false sign of hunger.

One of the most common false signs of hunger is a craving. Cravings usually come in waves that last about 20 minutes; so move away from the kitchen, biscuit tin or whatever else is tempting you, and distract yourself by doing something else. Maybe go for a short walk or make a phone call. This would also be a perfect opportunity to do the breathing exercise that you learned in the first chapter of this book (see page 65). As many people confuse hunger with thirst (in other words, you feel hunger when your body is, actually, telling you that it's thirsty), it's worth having a big glass of water to see if this takes away the desire to eat.

By doing something different you will start to recognize and break the automatic patterns of behaviour. Every time you successfully beat a false sign of hunger, you can put a coin in your *Sort Your Life Out* jar.

Whether you are over- or underweight, this tool is critical in helping you to reach and maintain a healthy body weight. One of the main reasons for this is that many people ignore their natural hunger signals during the day (often because they're busy) and then eat most of their day's intake in the evening, when their body least needs it. Many of us eat a lot of food in the evening, and then plop down in front of the TV before bed. So rather than use up the energy from our food, our bodies store it as fat cells. By eating sensibly throughout the day and listening to your true hunger needs, you can learn to eat just the right amount of food at the right times.

By eating only when your body genuinely needs food (and not for any other reason) you will re-establish a rapport with your body's needs and reverse the pattern of overeating and storing excess fat. When you practise eating only when your body needs food, you'll start to enjoy the feeling of being in touch with yourself and may even find that you get more pleasure from eating than you used to. You may notice that you no longer eat a set pattern of breakfast, lunch and dinner. Why? Because you aren't actually hungry, and your body doesn't actually need refuelling. For this reason, I suggest you carry a healthy snack with you when you're out and about – maybe some dried fruit and nuts – so that you have something nutritious to hand when hunger does strike.

From time to time, you may find yourself eating for reasons other than physical hunger. Use these as opportunities to assess *why* you are eating, and get to grips with what your personal 'eating triggers' might be. Above all, be patient with yourself and be prepared to muck up now and again. Remember that we were all born with the ability to eat only when we're hungry, so you can and will be able to do this. Congratulate yourself every time you eat only when you're hungry, and every time you stop when you've had enough.

QUICK CHECK

- How often do I eat when I'm not physically hungry? (10 = all the time; 1 = never)
- How much do I need to use this tool? (10 = very much so; 1 = not at all)

Use the relaxation and transformation tool

This is one of the best tools that you can use, and I would encourage you to do so every day. For many years I've been using this approach and have put together CDs that reinforce the messages of my programmes, and help people to relax. You'll find my mp3 relaxation tool at http://www.sortyour lifeout.com/book, where you can download it for free; simply click on the link that says 'Relaxation and Transformation mp3'. This mp3 track is an integral part of my weight-loss programme, www.petecohen.tv that is also available online. To take a free trial of this programme, visit http://sortyourlife out.com/book and click on 'Free Trial of petecohen.tv'. If you don't have access to a computer, ask a friend to download it for you, as it can be easily copied onto CD.

This mp3 track has been put together to help and support you as you reinforce all the behaviours that will help you to become healthy and fit. It will also help you to de-stress, so you will probably find that you want to continue listening to this well beyond the end of the 21 days. When you listen to this recording consistently, it will help consolidate your changes and you will find yourself feeling very relaxed, motivated and excited about changing. You will also experience how powerful your mind can be in giving you positive suggestions that reinforce the new behaviours you're taking on.

The reason I have included this is that I have found over the years that many people who are relaxed tend to be calmer and more in control of their emotions, and this gives them a better quality of life. People find that as they become more relaxed they don't feel the need to overeat or do other un-healthy things, and they also become better at dealing with what life throws at them. If you feel that you would benefit from being more relaxed, but are not able to download the mp3 track, or would like to use another tool, use tool 3, from Chapter One (Be Comfortable at Home, page 62). This is all about breathing and will make a huge difference to the way you feel.

Note: When you listen to the track, make sure you are sit-ting as comfortably as possible, in a quiet place where you won't be disturbed for about 25 minutes. Also, do not listen to it when you're driving, operating machinery or doing some-thing that requires your full attention.

QUICK CHECK
- How often do I set time aside to relax? (10 = every day; 1 = never)
- How important is this tool for me? (10 = very; 1 = not at all)

Avoid sugar, alcohol and caffeine

Sugar, alcohol and caffeine undermine your health and increase your weight. They also tend to form a large part of our diets, which makes them potentially all the more danger-ous. Let's look at why we need to cut these from our lives.

SUGAR

We are a nation addicted to simple sugar. In 1915, the average sugar consumption (per year) was around 15 to 20 pounds (7–9kg) per person. Today, the average person eats his or her body weight in sugar, which is closer to 150 to 200 pounds (68–90kg). When I talk about sugar, I am also talking about the kind of carbohydrates that are commonly referred to as 'simple carbohydrates', or those that have a high glycaemic index. If you aren't familiar with the latter term, a glycaemic index (or GI) ranks carbohydrates according to their effect on our blood glucose levels. High GI foods send blood sugar levels soaring, only to let them crash soon thereafter, while low GI foods produce a sustained form of energy that keeps blood sugar levels stable. High GI, simple carbs include white bread, rice, pasta and processed cereal, such as cornflakes and the sugar-coated cereals that children tend to love to eat. So, why are sugary foods and simple carbohydrates so bad for us?

Well, these foods provide empty calories. They don't contain any nutrients, such as fibre, minerals or vitamins, proteins, slow-release (low GI) carbohydrates or healthy fats. When we eat too much of them, our body has to use up stores of nutrients to digest them; but, because these foods don't replace the nutrients they use, we are left depleted of vitamins and minerals. Some nutritionists think that sugar and simple carbohydrates are so harmful that they even liken them to a drug.

How addicted are you? Answer the following questions to see how dependent you are upon sugary foods:

- Do you add sugar to foods and drinks, such as tea, coffee and breakfast cereals?
- Do you eat sugary snacks several times a week (e.g., biscuits, chocolate, cakes and sweets)
- Do you drink many soft or fizzy drinks each week?

- Do you always eat 'white' products, such as white bread, pasta or rice?
- Do you crave sugar when you're tired?
- Do you like to end a meal with something sweet?
- Do you always have sweet 'treats' in the house?

If you answered 'yes' to any of these questions, you will benefit from practising this tool, whatever your weight. If you are happy with your weight, you can experience health benefits, such as improved sleep and higher energy levels from cutting out sugar. And if you want to put on weight, by not filling yourself up on empty sugary calories, you can build up healthy tissue by eating more nutritious foods.

So why do we eat so much sugar? Sugar makes food taste good and it also makes us feel great, but we don't need it at all. And, even if sugar does give us a few minutes of pleasure, the long-term effects on our health can be serious. When we eat food that contains sugar or that gets turned into sugar very quickly in the body, we get a quick surge of energy. However, this causes our bodies to release a hormone called insulin, which subsequently causes our energy levels to crash. This can lead to health problems, such as Type 2 diabetes, headaches or migraines, tooth decay, poor immunity, yeast overgrowth (candida), skin breakouts, lack of concentration, mood swings and, of course, obesity.

Sugar and sugary foods are addictive, so I suggest you cut them down or even cut them out, for 21 days. This will allow you to break your dependence and reset your body to its natural state. You may not realize you're addicted, so hopefully over the next few days you'll have the chance to see just how much you rely on sugar for taste, comfort and/or energy. The only part of our bodies that needs sugar for fuel is the brain, and it only needs two teaspoons (10ml) at any one time. Even then, the brain doesn't need this fuel to come from sweet foods, as it can extract glucose by breaking down healthier carbohydrates such as fruit, vegetables, wholegrain pasta and bread, and brown rice.

What do you have to do? You can either start by cutting down your sugar intake and *then* cut it out for the 21 days; or, if you're feeling brave, you can cut it out for 21 days straight.

- Cut down the amount of sugar you add to your food or drinks
- Avoid foods containing added sugar, such as cakes, biscuits, soft drinks, sweets and chocolate
- Avoid simple carbohydrates (i.e., any 'white' pasta, bread and rice)
- Check your food labels for 'sugar', 'honey' and anything ending in '-ose', such as glucose, galactose, maltose, as these are all forms of sugar. The exception is fructose, as this naturally occurring sugar (found in fruit, for example) provides a steadier release of energy, contains some nutrition, and does not have the harmful effects of refined sugar
- Where possible, remove all sweet foods from your home
- Avoid artificial sweeteners, as they don't allow you to retrain your taste buds

Be prepared: When you make a change like this to your diet, it's important to be well prepared so that when you feel genuinely hungry, you have a healthy snack to hand so that you won't be tempted to grab something sugary. Good options include fresh fruit, nuts, oatcakes, cheese and raw vegetables. Visit http://www.sortyourlifeout.com/book, where you can download recipe ideas, or stop into your local health-food shop to investigate the wide range of interesting sugar-free snacks on offer.

Dealing with withdrawal symptoms: The initial stages of giving up sugar can lead to withdrawal symptoms and cravings, so it's a good idea to prepare yourself with a number of ways to distract yourself from the craving: ring up a friend, send an email, file your nails, go for a walk, brush your teeth, clean the bathroom, do some ironing, have a cup of herbal tea, relax in a bubble bath, meditate, listen to your favourite song or practise the breathing exercise on page 65. Only you know what will work for you, so make a list of distractions and keep it where you can easily see it.

ALCOHOL

Alcohol may be legal and socially acceptable, but it is also an addictive and toxic substance. It can cloud our judgement and make us do things we regret, damage our health and upset blood sugar levels. It has no nutritional value, and, because we often lose our inhibitions (and our judgement!) when we've had a few drinks, we can end up eating less healthy food, leading to a double-whammy of unhealthy behaviour. Some nutritionists and health experts argue that moderate amounts of alcohol, particularly red wine, are good for our health; however, because *Sort Your Life Out* is about reprogramming behaviour, I would like you to cut down or cut out alcohol for 21 days, to reset your habit patterns.

As with sugar, you have a choice of either cutting it out or reducing how much you drink for 21 days. If you are going to drink a little, here are some tips on how to keep your intake moderate:

- Consume a glass of water for every alcoholic drink you have
- Don't drink on an empty stomach
- Never use alcohol to quench thirst, as it only dehydrates you
- Be aware of how alcohol is making you feel and how much you've drunk. You many find it easier to do this at certain points in an evening; for example, every half an hour, or after each drink
- Drink at the pace of the slowest person in the room
- Be aware that measures of alcohol vary greatly. For example, nowadays, many pubs and restaurants serve glasses of wine that are 8oz (250ml), which, for a strong wine, can be up to three units
- Decide on a certain number of drinks in advance – i.e., I will only drink two glasses of wine or two half pints of lager – and then stick to it
- Buy high-quality alcohol and drink less of it

CAFFEINE

Caffeine is a stimulant found in tea (although not herbal and fruit teas), coffee, chocolate, cola and other caffeinated soft drinks. The aim is either to cut it out or reduce your intake to less than 2 small cups a day. Caffeine affects blood sugar in a similar way to sugar, in that it destabilises it and in the long term can affect the way in which our insulin functions. It's also addictive and has been linked to headaches, PMS and other health problems.

When you stop drinking caffeine, you may get some unpleasant reactions, such as headaches, irritability, lack of energy and grumpiness. But these withdrawal symptoms will pass after a day or so, so hang on in there. If you're used to having regular tea or coffee breaks or you're just used to boiling the kettle, drink herbal or fruit teas. Rooibos, or red bush tea, is a caffeine-free African tea that is fairly similar to black tea, and you can also buy coffee alternatives, such as dandelion root coffee, in heath-food shops. While you might find these a bit bland to start with, your taste buds will soon get used to their freshness and lightness. Why not be adventurous and try something you wouldn't usually have?

WHY ARE YOU DOING THIS?

Remember, I'm not asking you to cut the caffeine indefinitely. The next 21 days are about you taking control of your habits and resetting your brain to a new way of behaving that will help you become healthier. You may be one of those people who currently wakes up in the morning and thinks, 'I need my coffee', or maybe you get to mid-afternoon and think, 'I've got to have a sugar fix'. When you are stressed, you might say, 'I must have a drink to chill out'. Well, you might 'want' sugar, alcohol and caffeine, but you simply don't 'need' them. After 21 days, both your mind and body will have recalibrated themselves and you may find that you either don't want as much as you used to, or that you no longer want them at all. To reward yourself for not giving in to the temptation, remember to 'pay' into your *Sort Your Life Out* jar!

QUICK CHECK

- How toxic is my diet? (10 = I have lots of sugar, alcohol and caffeine; 1 = I don't have any sugar, alcohol or caffeine)
- How much do I need to use this tool? (10 = definitely; 1 = not at all)

Eat natural food

Apparently, there are now as many obese people in the world as there are those who are starving. The obvious difference between these groups is that one is overeating and one is undereating; however, the not-so-obvious similarity is that both are malnourished. While those of us in the developed world have more than enough to eat, the food we're eating is less nutritious than it used to be, partly because it is refined, pumped full of preservatives and other additives, and travels long distances to our shelves. We also lead more stressful lives than we used to and our bodies need even more vitamins and minerals to help us recover from stress. We are suffering both from how we live, what we eat and what we don't eat.

Every process that takes place in our body (such as digestion, fat burning, thinking, breathing, walking and talking) requires vitamins and minerals. If we fill up on junk foods, processed foods, sugary foods, deep-fried foods and takeaways, we deplete our bodies' stores of nutrients. If we don't replenish our stores, over time, we suffer from poor immunity and, ultimately, ill health. We find it harder to concentrate and process information, we have less energy, and we find it more difficult to metabolize food and burn fat. The good news is that we can reverse this process. When we eat fresh, natural foods, we top up our stock of vitamins and minerals, and get things going again.

IT'S ALL ABOUT CHOICE

Let's imagine for a minute or two that it's mid-afternoon and you are hungry. You fancy a snack, and you have two choices: an apple and a chocolate bar. What does each option give you? The apple will give you a steady release of energy; vitamin C, which is good for your skin, bones, blood and immunity; potassium, which helps to regulate your water balance, blood pressure and your heartbeat; and fibre, which keeps your digestive system healthy and helps reduce the risk of colon cancer. The chocolate bar, on the other hand, will give you a sugar hit, which will cause your energy levels to crash, and saturated fat, which increases your risk of heart disease. So, basically nothing of any value. When you look at food in this way, don't you think there's little competition between the natural and the highly processed?

Many people simply don't realize that packaged and processed foods do not provide the necessary nutrients to be healthy. It's not surprising, really, when many manufacturers give processed and packaged food ranges misleading names like 'healthy eating' or 'be good to yourself'. Food manufacturers refine and process foods to make them last longer and be more profitable, but in doing so they strip most of these foods of their key nutrients and health-giving properties. You deserve better than that. No matter what you might think about your body, or how long you've been abusing it with poor-quality food, your body deserves to have fresh, nutritious, natural food. So by focusing on eating natural foods and eliminating processed foods from your diet for 21 days, your body will detoxify and get used to foods that are gentle on your digestive system. You will also reduce your cravings and dependency on processed foods, and you might even find that by the end of the 21 days, you're enjoying foods that are different from the ones you used to eat.

HOW TO CLEANSE YOUR DIET

The foods that I suggest you limit or cut out for 21 days are:

- Processed ready meals
- Takeaway and fast foods
- Ready-made salad dressing (including low-fat and fat-free varieties)
- White flour, such as biscuits, cakes, white bread, etc.
- Sugary or processed cereals
- Deep-fried food
- Fatty processed meats, such as salami and ham
- Full-fat dairy products, such as milk, butter and cheese. Even though these are natural foods, they are very high in saturated fat, which can lead to raised cholesterol and higher risk of heart disease. You can still choose reduced fat varieties, such as skimmed milk or low-fat live natural yoghurt
- All refined sugars, caffeinated drinks and alcohol (see page 94)
- Diet drinks made with artificial sweeteners

LIMITING YOUR MISTAKES

I know that there'll probably be at least one occasion when you eat something that you know isn't good for you. But don't beat yourself up about it; instead, learn from the situations where this occurs. Notice how you feel and what you were thinking that made you want to eat that food in the first place. By becoming aware of your physical, mental and emotional triggers, you'll be able to avoid doing it again. While I suggest you try to plan very little for these 21 days, you may find that you are in a situation where you have little control over what you're eating (for example, you're staying with friends), simply try to limit your portions. If you don't draw attention to it, chances are other people won't either.

One technique that many people find useful in turning down food is simply to say, 'No thanks, I'm not hungry'. On the whole, other people don't have an argument against this (unlike things like 'I'm on a diet' or 'I've given up cakes') and it often makes them think about why they are eating, too! Saying that you aren't hungry works particularly well in situations where people are eating food for the sake of it – for example, puddings at mealtimes, birthday cake at work, or chocolate biscuits during a coffee break. And if you think you're really going to offend someone – for example, if they've made something special – then you can always take some away to eat later.

When you use this tool, you'll discover a new-found respect for food and for the joy it can bring into your life. Good food has colour, texture, taste and smell, and as well as being essential for life, eating is a full-body pleasure experience. So why not treat this experience as the chance to reconnect with your body's needs and natural sources of pleasure?

QUICK CHECK
- How natural is my diet? (10 = super natural; 1 = not at all)
- How important is this tool for me? (10 = very; 1 = not at all)

Drink water

Water is essential to life. It makes up between 55 and 75 per cent of our body weight, and we need it for many critical body functions, including temperature control, joint lubrication, removal of toxins, concentration and brain function, and digestion, among others. With so many important processes relying on a steady supply of water, it's not surprising we don't feel great if we let ourselves become dehydrated. On average, we lose about 3 pints (1.5 litres) of water a day – through the skin by sweating, via the lungs through our breathing, and through normal elimination. Some signs that you need a good drink are lack of concentration, headaches, dry mouth and skin, weakness, dizziness, hunger and, of course, thirst.

How much water do you drink every day? Do you drink the recommended 4 pints (2 litres)? You may think you drink enough water (as many people do) but if I asked you what colour your urine is, would you be proud to tell me that it's very pale yellow or nearly clear, or would you be embarrassed to admit that your urine is a dark yellow or orange colour?

HOW TO DRINK MORE WATER

Here are some tips to help you increase your water intake:

- Drink a glass of water as soon as you wake up
- Drink water whenever you have an alcoholic or caffeinated drink or, better still, instead of one
- Carry a bottle of water with you at all times, so you can keep track of how much you are drinking
- Drink little and often – your body can better absorb smaller regular amounts of water so if you do this rather than gulp lots in one go, you won't need to run to the loo every few minutes
- Eat lots of fresh fruit and vegetables, as they are a valuable, natural source of water
- If you think you might be hungry and not thirsty, have some water then see how you feel 20 minutes later
- Set an alarm (on your mobile phone or watch, for example) to go off every 30 minutes as a reminder to have a sip
- Remember, once you notice your mouth is dry, you're already dehydrated. Drinking little and often will prevent this from happening

QUICK CHECK

- How many glasses of water do I drink in a day? (10 = none; 5 = 4–6 glasses; 1 = at least 8 glasses)
- How important is this tool for me? (10 = very; 1 = not at all)

Tool 7

Walk for 30 minutes a day

 Walking is the best possible exercise. Habituate yourself to walk very far.
Thomas Jefferson

If you're currently inactive and you want to improve your general health and wellbeing, this tool is definitely one that will help you. Walking is one of the most underrated forms of exercise, and its impact on your health can be profound. You don't need any skill, and the only equipment you'll need is a comfortable pair of shoes. Better still, you can do it whenever and wherever it suits you.

There may not be anything ground-breaking about walking, and most of us take it for granted. However, in keeping with the *Sort Your Life Out* principle of making things habitual and easy to fit into your life, walking is something that pretty much everybody can do. It's so simple, and the health benefits are amazing. Regular walking:

- Burns fat
- Builds muscle, and so speeds up your metabolism
- Reduces the risk of heart disease, diabetes, stroke and several forms of cancer
- Helps reduce the risk of osteoporosis
- Releases endorphins, the body's natural painkillers
- Helps reduce stress

WHAT DO YOU NEED TO DO?

To maximize these benefits, ideally you need to walk at a moderate pace for 30 to 60 minutes every day. You should start by walking at an easy warm-up pace for 5 to 10 minutes; then, once your muscles are ready, you can increase your pace to a level where you're starting to breathe a little heavily (but should be able to hold a conversation).

Over time, as your body gets used to walking, your fitness levels will increase so you'll need to increase your pace to continue experiencing the benefits. Alternatively, to challenge your body, you can carry some special walking arm weights or a backpack containing weights, or you can simply walk for longer. When you finish your session, safely slow down your pace before you finish completely so that you give your body a chance to cool down. It probably goes without saying, but for the sake of safety, please wear bright clothes and/or walk with a partner, if you walk at night.

NO EXCUSES

If, after all that, you still think you can't fit walking into your day, here are some tips to help you make it a routine:

- Get up earlier or walk in the evening instead of watching TV
- Park your car further away from your destination
- Walk instead of taking the bus or train to work (or at least some of the way)
- Walk during your lunch break
- Schedule a walk into your diary
- Find people to walk with, so you stick to your commitment

Remember to 'log' your walks into your *Sort Your Life Out* journal and to put a coin into your jar every time you walk.

QUICK CHECK
- How many minutes a day do you walk? (10 = none; 5 = 15 mins; 1 = at least 30 mins)
- How much difference will this tool make for me? (10 = lots; 1 = none)

Do two to three activity sessions a week

We have joints, muscles, a heart, lungs, a sense of balance and coordination, all of which come together to help us be active. And being active, in turn, helps us to keep healthy. Regular activity is particularly beneficial for anybody who wants to lose weight, because it helps to boost the metabolic rate, which is critical for burning fat.

WHAT DO YOU NEED TO DO?
I'm suggesting you do two to three activity sessions a week, and to make sure that each session is, at the very least, comprised of 20 to 30 minutes of continuous movement that keeps your heart rate elevated throughout. Obviously, the more active you are, the more benefits you'll get, especially when it comes to losing weight, because you need oxygen to burn fat. The best way to raise your oxygen levels is through continuous rhythmical activity that gets your lungs and heart working. This is also known as aerobic exercise, and includes

swimming, jogging, cycling, walking, aerobics, aquarobics, dancing, tennis, squash and even some Wii exercises. Basically, you are looking for anything that gets you moving, out of breath and sweating. It's also great to do different exercise, so why not try as many things as you can to see what you enjoy the most and what fits well into your life?

One type of exercise that I *would* suggest you try is resistance training, which means toning your muscles using weights, exercise bands or your own body weight. Resistance training is often associated with serious athletes and bodybuilders, but for us laymen, it's also great for supporting the spine and improving posture, raising metabolism, and reducing the risk of developing osteoporosis in women. Some people also find that they feel more confident when they start doing this kind of exercise. If you are unsure of what to do, you could book a few sessions with a personal trainer (either in the gym or at home), who can show you exercises. You don't need to spend a lot of money (in fact, if you already belong to a gym, you'll likely get all the advice you need free of charge) and you also don't need to commit to seeing a trainer for a long period of time. If you explain that you want to be shown some resistance exercises that you can do on your own, most good trainers will be happy to help you out.

NO EXCUSES

Those who do not find time for exercise will have to find time for illness.
Earl of Derby

If one of the things that puts you off exercising is the fact you're not very fit, you'll be amazed at how quickly your fitness levels increase once you start exercising regularly. So, you may have to go through a bit of discomfort, but just think back to our arm-crossing exercise right at the start of this book; once you make exercise a routine in your life, you won't have to feel out of shape for long.

Just remember one thing: it's extremely difficult to motivate yourself to exercise if you keep making excuses. The most common excuse is 'I haven't got time', but the truth is, if you enjoyed exercising, you'd make the time, just as you find time for the other parts of your life that bring you pleasure. My job is to help you to find things that you truly enjoy.

GET MOTIVATED!

Most of us consider exercise to be something that involves hard work, and long, boring hours spent in a gym or on a track. But there are, in fact, some great ways to motivate yourself to exercise. Why not:

- Commit to meet a friend (either at the park or at the gym), or even set this up as a weekly event
- Promise your child/children to do something active with them; once you've told them you're going to do it, they won't let you go back on your word
- Sign up in advance for a class
- Combine exercise with socializing; i.e., instead of meeting a friend for a pint or a coffee and slice of cake, why not suggest a game of squash or a power walk around the park?
- Try a group exercise that can add a new dimension of

fun to your routine, such as ball sports or even group dance sessions

- Sign up for a charity event, such as a 5km run or a long cycle ride, and stick to the training plan you are given
- Focus on the feeling you're going to get when you've finished exercising – the glow and buzz you feel when you've been working hard and with that feeling in mind, get moving!

For every session you complete, you can add coins to your *Sort Your Life Out* jar. As they begin to mount up, you'll be even more motivated to continue. Think of something you want to buy with the money, and also see each coin representing a bit of weight lost or some fitness gained.

QUICK CHECK

- How many exercise sessions do I do each week? (10 = none; 1 = 3 or more)
- How much do I need to use this tool? (10 = very much so; 1 = not at all)

Be as active as you can

As well as finding time to do two or three scheduled exercise sessions, you can burn up lots of calories and improve your fitness simply by moving more during the day. You may be surprised to discover how many opportunities there are to get little energy boosts when you're at work, at home, or out and about.

This tool is for everyone, but it is particularly useful for people who may not want to join a gym, or those who have, perhaps, suffered from poor health and have to be careful with physical activity. As a nation we've become very inactive and we spend lots of time sitting down looking at our TVs or our computers. By shifting your lifestyle to incorporate more movement, your health will be affected on all levels. So, let's see how active you currently are:

- Do you use the remote control every time you change the TV channel?
- Do you always use a lift or an escalator instead of the stairs?
- If you're driving, do you always park your car as close as possible to your destination?
- How often do you carry your shopping home from the shops?
- Do you do your own housework?
- Do you always send emails to colleagues in your office, even when you could walk to see them?

Be honest when you answer these questions. You may even want to write down the answers in your *Sort Your Life Out* journal, so that there is no getting away from the truth. The health benefits of being more active are endless, and once you start experiencing them, you'll be motivated to continue moving. Among other things, being more active:

- Reduces the risk of premature death
- Reduces the risk of developing heart disease

- Reduces high blood pressure, and the risk of developing it
- Reduces high cholesterol, and the risk of developing it
- Reduces the risk of developing colon and breast cancer
- Reduces the risk of developing Type 2 diabetes
- Helps to build and maintain healthy muscles, bones and joints
- Lifts mood and energy levels

The goal is to fit as much activity into your daily life as possible. So wherever possible, walk to the shops, use stairs instead of escalators or lifts, park a bit further away when you go out in your car, get off the bus or train one stop from where you're going, or simply dance around to your favourite songs. Whenever you get the chance to be active, grab it, and then record your session in your journal and pop a coin into your *Sort Your Life Out* jar.

QUICK CHECK

- How active is my life? (10 = extremely; 1 = not at all)
- How much do I need this tool? (10 = very much so; 1 = not at all)

How to get the most out of this programme

Record your progress

Regardless of your goals, I suggest you record everything you do in your *Sort Your Life Out* journal. This will help you to get a clear idea of what works and what doesn't work so well for you. You can also keep a track of how well you're doing by remembering to put a coin into your *Sort Your Life Out* jar every time you practise a new behaviour.

Be patient

We live in a world where we want instant results and gratification. Once we've made the decision to make some changes, we want to feel healthy *right now*. We want our excess pounds to disappear overnight, or we want to be fit enough to run a marathon tomorrow. But as much as you might want these or similar things now, I want you to realize that the next 21 days are far more important than the result. The key thing is that you practise the tools until they become ingrained behaviour. It's a bit like playing Snakes and Ladders every day for 21 days; to get really good at the game, you need to learn which ladders to climb and which snakes to avoid.

In addition, I would suggest that you don't rush into this part of the programme. A lot of people do things out of desperation and so dash ahead without preparing. I want you to be in the best state possible when you start the 21 days, so please make sure you're ready. You may also want to find three weeks when you don't have any big social events as these can throw you off course. Equally, however, if you do have a day when you really can't use the tools, don't count that day as one of your 21, and carry on the following day.

Please remember that you don't have to use all of the tools. Depending on the state of your health, you may only need to do one tool consistently to see a huge difference. For example, if you're obese and don't currently drink any water, you will make significant changes just by drinking eight glasses of water a day. This will help your body metabolize fat better and also help you regulate your hunger. Or, if you haven't exercised for ten years, one walk a day will make a huge difference to the way you feel and your overall health. However, the more you do – properly and consistently – the more benefit you'll see.

What most people do is start with two or three tools (usually the ones they feel are most important for them), and then, once they've mastered these and they feel like habits, they start two or three more. Gradually, the advice will become automatic so by the time you have worked through all the tools you want to and have practised them over and over again, you will have a new lifestyle that will help you maintain the fitter, slimmer and healthier you.

The number 21 is a guideline

Although this was mentioned at the end of the last chapter, I think this is so important that I want to say it again. While this is a 21-day programme, you may find, as people often do, that you pick up some of the tools very quickly. For example, lots of people find that they get the hang of eating only when they're hungry after a few days of practising it. You may also find that some tools take longer to crack – and that's OK too. In some cases, you'll be undoing years of conditioned behaviour. The number 21 can also apply to the number of times you practise something, rather than 21 days. So, you may get the hang of something by undertaking a tool 21 times, and feel confident enough to move on to another tool. You may eat only natural food for a week, but if you are eating three meals a day, you've managed to get it right 21 times, which may well be just enough to settle your new behaviour in your brain. The key thing is that, however long it takes you, you repeat these tools until they become habits.

Measure your success

If your focus is weight loss, the best way to measure your success is not only by looking at your weight but also by taking body measurements, at your chest, waist and hips, for example. Weigh yourself a maximum of once a week and don't get obsessed with what the scales say; there are so many other ways of looking at your success. In fact, another good way to measure your success, even if you don't want to lose weight, is to rate how well you use these tools. You can do this on a scale of 1 to 10 (with 1 being not at all and 10 being completely), and the more often and the more tools you use, the more changes you will experience.

Sometimes it helps to get a little support, and to share your experiences with others in the same situation. Why not visit http://www.weightlossjournals/petecohen.tv, and use this to record your progress. Although this site was designed for people who are focused on losing weight, anybody can use the progress-reporting tool to get encouragement and find out how other people are doing. This will put you in contact with other people who are going through a similar process of change, and many people feel that the support they get, and the reassuring feeling that they are not alone, helps to keep them motivated and focused.

If your primary focus is to lose weight and you feel like you would enjoy a little one-to-one support and coaching, I can help you out. Visit http://www.petecohen.tv for a 50 per cent discount off my online weight-loss programme. Use the promotional code 'SYLO book' to gain this reduction. If you do this, you will have me as your own interactive personal coach every single day. If you aren't sure this is for you, sign up for a free trial first.

Check with your doctor

If you haven't exercised for a long time or have any concerns about your health, please consult your GP before starting the programme.

DAY:

TOOLS I'M USING TODAY:

*

*

*

*

*

THOUGHTS, FEELINGS AND OBSERVATIONS:

*

*

*

*

*

3 POSITIVE THINGS THAT HAPPENED TODAY:

*

*

*

ANY OTHER NOTES E.G. FOOD/ACTIVITY DIARY:

SORT YOUR LIFE OUT:

Confidence and Self-Esteem

In 1957, a group of monks in Thailand had to relocate a large clay Buddha from their temple to a different location to make room for a new highway to Bangkok. It began to rain and the head monk decided to cover the sacred Buddha with a large canvas to protect it. Later that evening he went to check on it, shining his torch under the canvas to see if the Buddha was still dry. He noticed a gleam catch the light and wondered whether there might be something under the clay. Using a chisel and hammer, he started to chip it away. As he knocked off shards of clay, the gleam grew brighter and brighter. Hours later, the monk was standing face to face with an extraordinary solid-gold Buddha that measured 10 feet (3 metres) tall, and weighed over 2.5 tonnes. Experts believe that several hundred years earlier, when the Burmese army was about to invade Thailand, the monks of the time had

covered their precious golden Buddha with a coating of clay to protect it.

Many of us are like this golden Buddha. Our confidence is hidden away, waiting to be uncovered. It's natural and common for us to believe that we aren't confident, and that we were simply made this way, but the truth is that we all have the capacity to glitter, and we can all be more confident, no matter how we are feeling now. In fact, as you'll discover in this chapter, we are all born confident, but our natural confidence becomes tarnished by experience. We all have the ability to feel good about ourselves; we just need to rediscover it. And that's what this chapter is about. There is a lot to cover, so let's start digging for gold!

What is confidence?

According to the dictionary, confidence means 'belief in oneself and one's powers and abilities' and self-esteem means 'a realistic respect for oneself'. However, I think there are some important subtleties around these terms that are more difficult to explain.

When I think of the people whom I know to be truly confident, I see them accepting themselves regardless of what other people think of them. True confidence doesn't change across time or situations – it means having a deep sense that everything about us is fine just the way it is. This doesn't mean never feeling nervous or unsure of ourselves, because we all have times when we feel out of our comfort zone; however, these situations should not make us question whether we are good enough. When we have true confidence, we know that we *are* always good enough and so we allow ourselves to experience a wide range of things.

Confident people are comfortable in their own skins and they acknowledge not only their good points but also their imperfections. There is no getting away from the fact that all of us are both physically and emotionally imperfect. None of us has perfect features and bodies, and not one of us is always in a perfectly balanced emotional state. These imperfections don't make us 'bad' or 'worthless', they simply make us human.

If you looked closely at me, you would notice that my feet are disproportionately large for my body, I've got a very large nose, and the hair that is missing from my head is growing out of my nose and ears. It's obvious that I'm not physically perfect. I'm not mentally perfect, either; there are times when my emotions get the better of me and I have moments of insecurity, doubt and fear. Luckily these are just moments and not permanent states, but they're imperfections nonetheless. None of us can change the fact that we're imperfect because we'll always be that way, but we can break the pattern of how we feel about our weaknesses and learn how to accept ourselves just as we are.

Confidence is a habit

While it may not seem like it, feeling confident is a habit, just like any other. People who are happy in their own skin have usually practised being this way. They have a go at new things and voice their opinions, knowing that they might not always get things right. The secret is that they also know that it's OK to get things wrong. Ironically, by accepting their limitations and imperfections, they build up their self-esteem.

On the other hand, people who have low self-esteem tend to avoid being in situations where they risk getting things wrong; they don't try new things and so, rather than build their confidence, they start to believe that they can't survive out of their comfort zone. If you lack confidence in this way, your world shrinks because you feel as if you can't cope with different situations. For this reason, being confident is fundamental to changing your life.

Just as it is involved in learning any new behaviour, the brain is involved in creating the habit of being confident. Whatever you believe about how confident you are, your brain will always be looking for ways to validate that belief. If you have a negative belief, for example 'I'm not good enough', your brain will take every opportunity to point out everything that confirms that fact, whether it is something you do, things other people say, or thoughts that you might have.

On the other hand, if you feel that you are capable and confident, your brain will pay attention to the signals that confirm that you are good enough – whether those signals come from thoughts you have, things you do, or things that other people say. Basically, whatever you believe will be confirmed by your mind. If you regularly have self-defeating thoughts, you will probably believe that it's difficult to break free of any negative pattern of beliefs. Why? Because your brain is, quite literally, keeping hold of your habitual thought patterns. You can't escape the pattern, because it's become ingrained, and protected by your own brain. Your brain isn't out to get you! It simply can't tell a negative, destructive belief from a positive, supportive one. It simply reinforces what you think, because it wants to help you.

Your confidence in any situation stems from how much you've practised being that way. For example, if you feel comfortable driving, try to think back to the first time you got into a car. I'll bet you didn't always feel so confident! But after driving for a few weeks, months or years, you started to feel totally at ease behind the wheel. The same goes for other areas of your life. If you overcome nerves or negative beliefs, and literally retrain your brain through practice, you'll soon start to see and experience confidence in all areas of your life.

How confident are you?

Do you think you are confident? When you ask most people this question, they usually say that they are confident in some situations, but not in others. For example, they might feel confident at work, but not so confident when they have to wear a bikini on the beach; or they might feel confident with family and friends, but less so when they have to meet new people for the first time. It's not uncommon, either, to find people who feel that they completely lack confidence, because they are so used to feeling inadequate, they don't realize that there are definitely times when they are confident – even if it's only when they're on their own.

I want you to put this book aside for a couple of minutes and get out your *Sort Your Life Out* journal. Write down all the areas where you feel you lack confidence. Some most common examples of things I've seen include: giving presentations, meeting new people, negotiating, going to the gym, being on the beach and talking to the boss. There will be some things that are very personal to you, but remember that unless you choose to share this journal with anyone else, your notes are just for you. Write down everything you can think of, even if it seems a little silly.

I don't want you to dwell on these areas, but I'm hoping that by writing them down, you can step back from this list and see some of these behaviours in a different light. Often when I get people to jot down areas where they are insecure, they realize that in the grand scheme of things these areas are simply not important; or they even laugh at some because they see them as insignificant and nothing to get worked up about.

Now you've done that, I want you to write down all the times when you are confident. You can include 'big' things, such as giving presentations, organizing events, entertaining for large parties and being interviewed, but I also want you to focus on the 'little' things that people often overlook. These might include things like reading a bedtime story to your children, cleaning the house, parallel parking and gardening.

Because being confident is a habit that you can practise and improve, I want you to see that in this list there are probably many things about yourself that you take for granted – things for which you've probably never given yourself any credit. By writing them down, it's possible to see them in a new light – daily behaviours and routine events that, when you step back from them, all help to build a picture of you as a confident person. You don't have to bungee jump, start your own business or be the CEO of a top company to prove that you have a high sense of self-worth; everything you do, every day, is evidence of how you feel about yourself.

We were all born confident

In negative periods of our lives, it may seem as though we have never been confident; however, the truth is that we were all born feeling great about ourselves. At a young age, we didn't know any other way of being. We didn't know what confidence was, or that it could be lost. We had no idea about self-esteem or what it meant to be self-conscious. We didn't particularly care what we looked like, or what other people thought of us. We didn't judge ourselves, and we didn't judge anybody else. We were just at ease in our own skins.

If you find this hard to believe, just watch a child under the age of three. Look at how they act and how naturally confident they are. While they may experience a little shyness for a few minutes when they meet someone new, they soon start enjoying themselves without being self-conscious. They simply get on with what they are doing and are often oblivious to the rest of the world.

As you may remember from my own story, however, children reach an age when they start mimicking grown-ups and that's how they learn to become self-conscious. Young children look up to their parents, teachers, relatives and other influential adults and tend to copy what they do. They are often spoken down to, and so develop feelings of being inadequate. They become sensitive to even the subtlest behaviours in the adults who surround them and because there aren't many confident role models from whom children can learn, they often end up learning how to feel inadequate instead. It's a legacy of insecurity that gets passed from generation to generation. This isn't usually done with any negative intent; it's just the way it is. So it's no wonder that, as adults, we lack confidence because of what we experienced when we were growing up; most of us were surrounded by people who lacked confidence themselves.

I am about to share with you some techniques that you can repeat over and over again, to teach your brain how to support you in a different way. You learn to be confident in much the same way that you learned not to be confident! You *can* feel more comfortable with who you are by practising confident behaviours. Every one of us has personal areas in which we would like to have a higher sense of self-esteem. I am not able to cover every specific situation in this book; however, what you will learn in this section of the programme are techniques that you can use to be more confident in any situation. Whether you want to feel comfortable asking for a pay rise, strutting on the dance floor, or delivering a speech, what you will learn will help you achieve your goal.

How can we learn to be confident?

We're not taught at school how to be confident, and not many of us were taught by our parents, either. But, it's never too late to learn and it's never too late to change the way you feel.

 Worrying is a lot like a rocking chair, it's something to do for a while but it doesn't really get you anywhere.
Van Wilder

So what do really confident people do? When someone is very good at doing something, they often don't know exactly what it is they're doing. They behave so unconsciously that if you ask them to teach you, they'd look confused. So what I have done over the last ten years is study what thoughts and behaviours confident people have that help them believe in themselves – no matter what.

You may remember me saying earlier that if you want to feel stressed, the best way to do it would be to copy some-one who is an expert at being stressed. Or, on a more positive note, if you want to get really fit and healthy, you could learn how to be that way by modelling the behaviour of someone who leads a healthy, active life. Basically you can learn to do anything by practising certain behaviours.

What's the worst that could happen?

Over many years of working with people, one thing that I have noticed about those who lack confidence is that they think the worst about the unknown. They imagine things to be really, really bad, and they find it hard to be realistic about what may or may not happen. This is different from confident people, who seem to be able to approach any situation with a balanced sense of perspective about what might happen.

When you are facing a challenging situation, one way in which you can start to have a more balanced view is to ask yourself: what's the worst that could happen? While it's not good to dwell on the worst thing, once you accept it from a realistic point of view you can then think about how you want things to turn out. Things are never usually as bad as we imagine, and the reality is likely to be a welcome relief!

Picture the event that you're worrying about and imagine in as much detail as you can doing really well. This is known as 'acting as if', and when you use this frame to create a compelling image of you being confident, you start to give your brain something different to focus on.

To practise this, I suggest that you run through this exercise right now for a situation about which you currently lack confidence. You can do this in your head, or you can write down your thoughts in your *Sort Your Life Out* journal. You may find it easier to focus on the exercise and clarify it by jotting things down.

So, think of a situation that you soon have to face – for example, giving a presentation, asking a relative for a favour, or negotiating a pay rise. First of all, ask yourself, 'what's the worst that could happen?' It may be that you feel embarrassed for five minutes, that your relative says 'no', or that you end up with the same money as before. None of these is an ideal situation, but none marks the end of the world, either.

People with low self-esteem tend to 'catastrophize', so they imagine everybody laughing out loud at them, people shouting at them or even losing their job. They find it hard to see the worst-case scenario in a realistic way, and instead fantasize a scenario where things go incredibly badly. I want you to keep a realistic sense of perspective about what could happen.

Once you have accepted a realistic worst-case scenario (which either usually lasts for a few moments or only leaves you in the same situation in which you started, so no worse off) you can now imagine the ideal scenario.

Readjust your thinking a bit. How would you act if you

were confident? How would you be moving? How would you be speaking? What would you be thinking? What positive messages would you be giving yourself?

By answering these questions, you have to put yourself in a confident state. The process of imagining what could happen if you were confident makes you 'act as if' you are already confident. The mind does not know the difference between something that you imagine very vividly and something that is real, so by imagining this over and over again, you can, in your imagination, change your reality.

People who are truly confident are not fearless, and they also don't believe that everything will go their way. What they do believe is that they can cope with the worst-case scenario and that it's worth taking a risk for the possible returns. So, if you really need some money and pluck up the courage to ask a relative, you might be daunted by the prospect of her saying 'no', but equally, if things go according to plan, she could say 'yes', and you'd be getting what you want. Positive risk-taking is an excellent way to make changes in your life, because if you aren't prepared to take some chances, change will be that much slower in coming. When you adopt the attitude that you *can* cope with the worst-case scenario, things do start to go your way because you believe they can.

The first sign of madness

I remember being on a self-development course in 1997, when the teacher kept talking about the importance of paying attention to our 'internal dialogue'. I distinctly remember saying to myself, 'I don't know what he's talking about. What is an internal dialogue?' It took me at least a month to work out what he'd been going on about, and that was when I realized that I talked to myself a lot of the time. I also realized that a lot of this chat was pointless, and a waste of time. So I have come to learn both through my experience and through working with others that the quality of our internal dialogue is critical to how we feel.

You may have heard that the first sign of madness is talking to yourself. The truth is that we all talk to ourselves, and many of us do so all the time. It's completely normal. What may not be so normal is the *way* in which we talk to ourselves. Most of us are intelligent enough to realize that in order to be healthy we need to eat well and look after our bodies, but few of us are intelligent enough to realize that what we put into our minds also needs to be healthy. In a nutshell, the quality of our lives comes from the quality of our communication with ourselves. If we speak to ourselves in a self-defeating, negative way, life will seem negative and draining. If our internal dialogue is supportive, enthusiastic and nourishing, life will be exciting, fun and upbeat. It really is as simple as that.

Shut the Duck up

Some of you will have heard me liken our internal dialogue to having a Duck in our head, which often quacks away. The Duck is that voice that can say negative things to you, such as 'you're not good enough', 'you're lazy', 'you can never change', 'you don't have any willpower', 'you're fat', 'you're unlovable', and so on... What does your Duck say to you? Many of the self-defeating things people say to themselves include:

- They won't like me
- I'll never be able to do that
- I'm wrong again
- I can't believe I did that
- I'm so stupid
- I'm too fat
- I wish I was…(clever/funny/popular/thin/rich, etc.)
- It's my fault
- I'm so annoyed with myself

If we tell ourselves anything enough times, we start to believe it's true. Similarly, if we say things to *other* people over and over, they'll start to believe in what they are being told. The difference is, of course, that we tend to say much nicer things to other people than we do to ourselves. For example, if you told a child over and over again that they were not good enough, they would eventually start to believe it. But we wouldn't do that to a child, because it's cruel or hurtful. The sad thing is that many of us have no qualms about speaking to ourselves in a self-defeating way – we're just not aware that we do.

Most people are not fully aware of what their Duck says to them and how much it dominates their internal dialogue. Later on I will be suggesting that you write down the things your Duck says. Once you are aware of what you're saying to yourself, you will be able to start changing this and maybe even begin to 'shut the Duck up'!

Take responsibility for yourself

In America, a man sued McDonald's, claiming that they were to blame for his weight problems. He said that the restaurant chain should have made it clear to him that the food they were serving was not healthy (as he had thought it was) and that it was this negligence on their part that caused his obesity and ill health. If this man is ever going to sort out his health issues, he will need to give up blaming McDonald's and become accountable for his situation.

Our culture is becoming increasingly blame-focused, with the popularity of suing people at an all-time high. Of course, it's within your rights to sue someone who's negligent, and there are definitely times when this is an effective and appropriate response. But for other situations, suing is just a way of assigning responsibility to someone else for our own misfortunes and the circumstances of our decisions. Owning a problem, and therefore the solution, is key to dealing with it. You need to become more accountable for the way you feel, and act with responsibility. How does this apply to being more confident? Read on...it has to do with forgiving yourself.

Forgive yourself

This may sound a bit strange and you may be wondering what I mean by this suggestion, so here is a short story that I think clearly explains my point.

Two monks were on a long walk, when they came to a stretch of water. There was a beautiful woman standing nearby, and she asked the monks to help her get across the water. The younger of the two monks lifted her up and carried her over the water, then he resumed his walk with the older monk. After a few minutes the young monk detected a sense of agitation and annoyance in the older monk, and asked him what was wrong.

'We are not allowed to look at or touch, let alone carry women,' said the older monk.

To which the young monk replied, 'I put her down on the other side of the water; you are still carrying her.'

In the process of becoming more confident in yourself, you need to let go of both the negative thoughts you have about yourself, and the negative ways in which you have been treating yourself. This short parable demonstrates in a simple yet, I think, effective way, how we can carry things with us even when they are of no use, or when they stop us from moving on in life. If you don't free yourself to act in a different way, you will end up doing what you've always been doing, and behave in a self-defeating way.

Many of us hold on to habits that we don't need. The secret to changing is to recognize the difference between what we need to hold on to and what we need to let go of. Some of the things that you will be letting go are self-defeating thoughts and destructive behaviours. They might seem like old friends, simply because you've had them for so long, but you have to forgive yourself, and let go of these to make room for new, healthier habits.

Children tend to be very good at forgiving, because they spend very little time mulling over the past; they think or feel something and then they move on. What most adults do is blame other people or blame themselves for what goes on in their lives. It's not helpful to blame anyone, even yourself. Blame is destructive, and it discourages us from taking personal responsibility. If we aren't able to take personal responsibility, we are equally unable to make changes. What is far more powerful is the ability to take responsibility for what you are doing to yourself; once you do this, you realize that everything you do to yourself is simply a habit and so, because you are in control of your habits, you can choose to change them whenever you want.

Forgiveness, to me, is about freeing yourself. It's not about the people who've hurt or taken advantage of you. You can't do anything about other people, or what goes on in their heads. You can, however, look after yourself and liberate yourself from the prison of your anger or resentment. There are huge emotional costs involved in allowing someone to have power over how you feel, because in doing this you relinquish control over yourself, which may lead to you feeling helpless and stuck. When you realize that nobody can make you feel a particular emotion, and that you can choose to move on from any negative event, even those caused by other people, then you can really allow yourself to change. It's time to wake up. If these feelings could be measured or weighed in some way, I'm sure you'd see just how much of a burden they are.

Accept the truth: you are amazing

I am, indeed, a king, because I know how to rule myself.
Pietro Aretino

Even if you've been telling yourself that you aren't good enough for a long, long time, this doesn't mean it's true. What is good enough? It is simply not true that you need to own certain items, look a certain way, earn a certain amount of money, or have a certain job to be good enough. There will always be things in your life that you won't have, or have yet to achieve, and you will always have shortcomings, both physical and mental. It is very important to recognize that you are *always* good enough. That is the truth. The sooner you accept your uniqueness, the easier it will be for you to become more confident. By being gentle with yourself, and appreciating all that you have and all that you are now, you will have a strong foundation on which to change your life for the better. You are amazing, and I'm going to help you find ways to become comfortable with that idea.

Body confidence

One of the most common areas where people lack confidence involves how they look. So, let's spend some time examining how you feel about your appearance.

Sadly, problems associated with low self-esteem and body image are starting at increasingly younger ages. Surveys often quote figures as high as 9 out of 10 women being unhappy with the way they look, and men are also becoming increasingly less content with their bodies, with growing numbers admitting to thinking about plastic surgery.

This pressure comes from the idealized body images that surround us. The pictures we see in magazines, on television, at the movies and on billboards are unattainable for almost everybody; however, this doesn't stop most of us from trying to pursue the dream of a perfect body. Most people would have to train in a gym for several hours a day, eat practically nothing, get some plastic surgery, and benefit from the judicious use of an airbrush to look like these media images of perfection. Not exactly achievable for the average person on the street, is it? It's no wonder we end up feeling unattractive and beat ourselves up for being 'too fat', 'too skinny' or simply 'ugly'. We're trying in vain to reach a state of perfection that doesn't actually exist.

Just take a moment to stand back and take a realistic view of this situation. If you spend some time wishing you were thinner, taller, shorter, broader, more muscle-bound, more toned or more beautiful, then you can feel comforted that you're not alone! The vast majority of people would like to look different, but most of us don't and won't ever have the perfect body and face.

The way in which you look at yourself dramatically affects the quality of your life, but some people find it hard to take body image seriously, because it can seem shallow. After all, we're about more than skin-deep beauty, aren't we? While this is most definitely true, body image is important. Why? Because poor body image leads to feelings of inadequacy, which can impact on so many more areas of life. Having a negative body image can reach the very core of your self-esteem, which means that if you don't like your body, you end up not liking yourself. And, in turn, if you don't like yourself, you will not believe that you're worth making an effort for.

For example, people who feel badly about themselves often don't feel motivated to take care of their bodies; they don't enjoy the intimate side of relationships, and they may feel inhibited, never taking chances or opportunities they are offered, because they don't think they are worth it. Nourishing yourself both inside and outside will not only help you to feel better about how you look, but also to feel good about how you treat and respect yourself.

Get real

Although it's not the whole answer, this simple exercise can help you start to see yourself in a different light. You don't have to show anyone what you write, so answer these questions honestly, even if you feel a bit uncomfortable saying positive things about yourself. Use your *Sort Your Life Out* journal to do this.

- List four things you like about your personality (e.g., I like the way I can talk to anyone. I make people laugh. I care about other people's feelings. I am generous. I am clever.)
- List four things a close friend might say they like about your appearance. If you're not sure, ask them! Ask them which bits of you are beautiful, strong, distinctive or admirable. You will probably find that what they say is very different from what you think.
- List four positive things you think about your body. If you find this hard to do, you can focus on really small things as a starting point (e.g., I have really soft hands. I have long luscious eyelashes. I have pretty feet. I have a lovely round bottom.)
- Think how you respond when someone pays you a compliment. Do you just brush it aside? Rejecting compliments can be upsetting not only for you but

also for the person giving the compliment. Practise accepting them simply by saying 'thank you'.

Accepting your body will make you feel better about yourself, and you'll be more inclined to look after your body and your health. It might sound like a cliché, but your body is the greatest thing you'll ever own; and you have the choice to criticize it or accept it for being amazing.

The quality of our lives comes down to how well we communicate with ourselves. Most of us beat ourselves up and put ourselves down; but if we can start to make the most of our bodies, we can feel different. If you are judging your body based on what you see in the media, or by comparing yourself with your friends, you are setting yourself up for failure. Rather than dwelling on your imperfections, acknowledge your personal characteristics and qualities, and make the most of them. Changing your attitude can change your life.

Confidence tools

As you may have guessed from reading this chapter, the key to having more confidence lies in learning to speak to yourself in a different way. So I suggest you use these tools for the next 21 days. By the end of that time, you will have started to programme a new way of seeing yourself.

A lot of people are frightened to look at themselves because they're worried about what they're going to discover. We're so used to not being aware of what we do and what we are thinking that when we turn the spotlight on our behaviour, we can feel a bit anxious. It's like clearing out your house and finding a cupboard that you know is a bit messy. If you want to clear it out, you have to open the door and see what's in there, and you also have to be prepared to find some dust, dirt and things you can't be bothered to sort out. To be happier and feel better about ourselves we have to go through a similar process, and that can sometimes cause a little discomfort. However, I think that the tools I'm about to share with you are gentle enough that you can get the same result and, at the same time, enjoy the process of becoming more self-aware.

The confidence journal

Most of us are not fully aware of how self-defeating our internal dialogue is, so first of all I want you to pay attention to what you say to yourself. This will give you the power to change it.

You can use your *Sort Your Life Out* journal for this exercise. I want you to be curious and interested about the messages you send to yourself on a daily basis. Write down some of the things that you say to yourself, and start to look for patterns. Include both the positive and negative comments that you make. Your diary may look something like this:

What I was doing	What I said	How I felt
Looking in mirror	Gosh, I look old	Old and tired
Cut someone up in traffic	I'm so stupid	Embarrassed and annoyed
Standing at school gates	I'm fatter than her	Frumpy and heavy
In meeting with boss	She thinks you're useless	Down and teary

This challenge is about being more aware of what you say to yourself without making judgements. Don't label anything 'good' or 'bad', just express some curiosity about the messages you give to yourself, and be aware of what they are. One way to do this is to imagine that everything you say to yourself is on speakerphone – that every thought you have can be heard by everybody. Would you be proud of what you broadcast to the world? To become more confident, you have to know what's currently preventing you from *being* confident. You need to become aware of what you are saying to yourself so that you can make some changes. What do *you* need to stop saying to *yourself* in order to feel great about who you are?

As you look back over your journal, you may well start to realize how silly it is to talk to yourself in a negative way. You may also see a pattern develop – certain times or situations in which you particularly lack confidence, or certain beliefs or sayings that you use more than others. I don't want you to judge yourself negatively when you do this (as that would defeat the object of the exercise), but I do want you to realize how silly this is. When I talked earlier on about keeping a sense of humour, I meant that I want you to try to make light of this exercise and then make the decision to change how you speak to yourself. The first step in doing this comes next.

Shut the Duck up

This has got to be one of my favourite exercises, because everybody can relate to it. You and I both know that we often speak to ourselves in a negative voice and give ourselves an unnecessarily hard time. By noting down in the first tool some of the things you say to yourself that are self-defeating, you now have some evidence of why you may have low self-esteem. So, to be more confident, you need to start talking back to the Duck.

Every time you notice that Duck saying negative things, tell it to 'Shut up!' You might think I'm joking, but I'm serious. This will break the pattern of your internal dialogue and, when you do this repeatedly, the Duck will eventually quieten down. By the way, you don't have to do this out loud, just talk back to the Duck in your head. To keep track of how well you're doing, every time you tell your Duck to shut up, put a coin in your *Sort Your Life Out* jar.

To remind you to do this, go to my *Sort Your Life Out* website, http://www.sortyourlifeout.com/book, where you can download a 'Shut the Duck up' picture to remind you to use this tool.

The mirror exercise

If you want to be more confident and feel better about your-self, it is really important that you learn to lighten up and not take yourself so seriously. One of the best ways to do this is to laugh and smile more. What I am going to suggest to you now might seem a little strange, but it works! I want you to look in the mirror and make ugly faces until you laugh. Don't just do this once – do it every day! You will probably choose to do this when you're on your own! When you have done this, replace that face with a smile and remember that it's almost impossible to lack confidence and self-esteem while you are smiling.

You may think I'm being silly, but the point of this tool is to realize that we're all a bit of a joke. And the sooner we realize that, the better. If aliens landed from another planet and looked at what we do to ourselves, they would probably think we were mad. I also think they'd probably laugh at how silly and pointless our behaviour can be. But while some of our actions can be painful, what we do to ourselves is often funny. I believe that when we can laugh at ourselves, we gain a sense of power and perspective that helps us to move on and change. By laughing, I don't mean ridiculing ourselves in a teasing way, as there isn't much to be gained from being harsh with ourselves. What I mean is not taking ourselves so seriously, and gently observing that a lot of our negative thought patterns don't serve any useful purpose. They may keep us in a familiar place but, for most of us, that familiar place is an uncomfortable one.

Be your own coach

Have you ever been coached for a skill or sport? Maybe you've had some tennis lessons, or you had someone help you with a musical instrument. Well, you can be coached in pretty much anything nowadays – including confidence.

So, if you wanted to find a coach to help you become more confident, what type of coach would you like? Would you want someone who gave you a hard time and shouted at you? Or would you like someone who respected you and was always encouraging and supportive? Chances are you would want someone who would give you positive words of encouragement, who would back you up no matter what, who could make you laugh, and who would see the positive side of any situation.

So I want you to imagine that you have employed a coach to help you boost your confidence and raise your self-esteem. Use your imagination and decide how you want them to be. Think about the following things:

- Is the coach male or female?
- What is their mission for you?
- What sort of voice do they have: loud, soft, calm, exciting or a combination?
- What sort of words do they use?
- How often do they speak to you?
- How do they make you feel?

Spend some time designing this coach – because it is going to be you! To build up your confidence, you need to encourage and support yourself.

This tool also links in with the Duck in your head. When you are coaching yourself in a positive way, the Duck won't be able to get a word in edgeways because you will quite literally talk over it. So, when you've told the Duck to shut up, you need to make sure you keep it quiet by replacing those old negative comments with nurturing ones from your coach.

This can be a challenging prospect for many people. Most of us are not used to being like this with other people, let alone ourselves. We're also unused to other people being that way with us. But just because this is a new way of being doesn't mean it has to be hard. Remember that the more you enjoy the process, the more likely you are to stick at it and see results. Why not see this technique as something fun and exciting?

 There is little difference in people but that little difference makes a big difference. The little difference is attitude. The big difference is whether it is positive or negative.
W. Clement Stone

Sort Your Life Out journal

DAY:

TOOLS I'M USING TODAY:

*
*
*
*
*

THOUGHTS, FEELINGS AND OBSERVATIONS:

*
*
*
*
*

3 POSITIVE THINGS THAT HAPPENED TODAY:

*
*
*

ANY OTHER NOTES E.G. FOOD/ACTIVITY DIARY:

SORT YOUR LIFE OUT:
Relationships

What's love got to do with it?

When someone asks me what I think about relationships, I think back to a long and, what was, at times, intense conversation I had with a good friend of mine. Let's just call him Tom. My friend Tom is of Asian descent and he grew up knowing that he would have an arranged marriage. At the time of our conversation, he had been very happily married for ten years, to a woman he had met only once before their wedding day. Those of us who don't belong to a culture that embraces arranged marriage can be very cynical about the concept and, yet, what my friend had to say makes a lot of sense. His view of marriage was that it was a partnership that operates much like a business. Both parties have an interest in getting along, settling disagreements as quickly as possible, and making the relationship happy and successful. They were not head-over-heels in love, and they didn't even choose each other, but by adopting this attitude, Tom experienced how love and mutual respect can grow out of open and honest friendship and companionship.

While not many of us belong to cultures where arranged marriage is the norm (and although not all arranged marriages work out), I think there is a lot we can learn from the mindset of couples who willingly enter into relationships like these. They tend not to chase a romanticized version of love, and therefore don't expect their relationships to be healthy without effort being invested in them. Rather, they believe that love blossoms through hard work and commitment, shared values and mutual respect. Regardless of religious or spiritual upbringing, I don't know many people who would disagree that these things are invaluable in any successful, loving partnership. And just imagine how fantastic a relationship could be if you were in love as well?

My parents tell a similar story about their own marriage. They had to learn through experience how to work at their marriage, and now they are not only best friends, but they also love each other more than ever before – and they've been together for nearly 50 years.

Stories like this prove that it is possible to create and stay in a happy and committed relationship, so this part of the *Sort Your Life Out* programme is about helping you to understand better the relationships in your life so that you can make them successful.

While I will touch on the relationships we have with our friends, family (including children) and colleagues, the focus of this chapter is intimate relationships, and how we can be successful at every stage of their life cycle. We'll look at how to choose the right partner, why relationships are so important to us, how to learn from your habitual patterns of behaviour in all relationships, how to maintain a long-term relationship, and, finally, how to end a relationship that is no longer right for you. I realize that nowadays there is no such thing as a typical relationship, and that there are many different partnerships and family set-ups, including cohabiting couples, single parents, dual breadwinners, blended families, inter-cultural relationships, female breadwinners and same-sex relationships. Each partnership has its own hurdles to overcome; however, you can be sure that the information in this chapter is relevant to all types of intimate partnerships.

Why are relationships so important to us?

In our society, we are sold the ideal that we will marry and live happily ever after. As children, our parents read us fairy tales to send us to sleep, leading us to believe that we will meet a beautiful princess or a handsome prince and ride off together into the sunset to enjoy a life of romance. Sadly, this is far from the norm.

There are several different meanings of the word 'relationship', but the two that stick out for me are 'a connection' and 'an involvement'. We are all inherently social beings, and each of us is the product of the individuals who have surrounded us physically, mentally and emotionally; therefore, 'connection' is the positive side of relationships. 'Involvement', however, is the more negative side of relationships. If we become 'involved' to an unhealthy degree with someone and their life, we can find it hard to maintain our independence and sense of self – and that's when relationships can become troubled.

A friend is one that knows you as you are, understands where you have been, accepts what you have become, and still, gently allows you to grow.
William Shakespeare

Great expectations

Relationship problems can arise when people fall into a partnership out of desperation – when they decide to be with someone because it seems better than being alone. In cases like this, people often 'choose' the wrong person – someone who is perhaps similar to a past partner – and they find themselves repeating the same patterns and issues that they had in their previous relationships. Alternatively, they look for partners who are similar to their parents, or the parents they never had.

It may not seem logical to go for the same kind of relationship, especially if it wasn't a happy one. Nor does it make obvious sense to look for someone to replace a parental figure. However, there is a reason why many of us do this. We often look to a partner to meet our unmet needs – the fears and desires that are hidden from our consciousness. This may not seem rational or sensible, but if we have unresolved issues in our lives, we will seek to sort them out by putting ourselves in the situation where they arise, and we'll keep doing this until we deal with the underlying problem.

For example, someone who gets unhealthily jealous because they have low self-esteem will often find that they attract partners who are very flirtatious. They feel deeply envious, and insecure about their relationship. The way that they need to sort it out is by becoming more secure and self-confident. Part of them knows that they need to do this to be happier in all areas of life and so this part of them draws to them people who bring up their jealousy in the hope that they'll finally deal with it. So they continually attract this kind of person until they resolve their security issues.

To avoid repeating painful patterns, we need to become aware of how we feel about ourselves, as well as the feelings we have about relationships, and the needs we have within them. This is the key reason why I emphasize the need to work first through Chapter One, before you move on to the remainder of the programme. You need to become aware of your imperfections and issues so that you can either work through them or, at the very least, try to avoid situations that make them worse.

Shortly, we'll move on to look at the patterns you follow when you are in a relationship; but, first of all, given that we know that relationships can be problematic, let's look at why we are motivated to have them at all.

Why do you want a relationship?

How many people do you know who don't feel complete unless they are in a relationship? How many people seem to long for security, constantly spending their time looking to be with someone, and feeling unable to face the world alone?

People who have this kind of attitude tend to have a poor relationship with themselves; that is to say, because they don't see how great life can be when they're on their own, they constantly search for someone else to fill in what they perceive to be gaps.

This view of being alone – as a wilderness that has to be endured – is very limiting. A healthier and more nourishing way to view being alone is to see it as an opportunity to do whatever you want, and to indulge yourself with people and experiences that make you most happy. Once you have done that and have got to know who you are, what you want and what you need, you can look for someone to complement you.

Ironically, it's often only when we're in a relationship that we realize the positive things about being single, and appreciate the freedom that comes with it. When we meet someone new, it's not uncommon to give up a lot of our time, energy and power, and it's equally common to stop viewing ourselves as a whole person in our own right. I recently worked with a lady who was a great example of this. She constantly referred to her partner as her 'other half' or her 'better half', and talked about herself only in terms of being part of a unit with him. What I wondered was, if her husband was her 'better half', what did that make her? The 'worse' or 'lesser half'?

Relationships build on the relationship we have with ourselves, and the more we invest in ourselves, the happier we can be when we share ourselves with someone else. When two people who clearly know who they are and who take great care of themselves come together, the possibilities for happiness, love and growth are endless.

The game face

When we face the world, most of us present a 'game face'. This is an emotional mask that hides what we're really feeling and/or thinking. In fact, sometimes, we are so good at masking our emotions that we even hide them from ourselves. However, to sustain healthy relationships, we have to be in touch with our feelings, and this relies on our being able to recognize when we're stressed. Whatever your personal situation, working through this next exercise will help you understand how the way in which you react to negative emotions affects how you interact with others.

Here are some quick questions for you to answer. Answer them honestly and thoroughly, as the more information you have, the more useful it will be:

- When I feel agitated, do I know how to calm myself quickly? If so, how do I do this?
- Can I easily let go of my anger? If so, how do I do this? If not, how do I feel when I keep hold of my anger?
- Can I turn to other people at work to help me calm down? If I do, how do I feel? If I don't, what do I do instead?
- When I come home at night or, if I work from/am at home, how do I feel at the end of the day?
- How do I interact with people who are stressed? Am I helpful to them? If so, how?
- When my energy is low, how, if at all, do I boost it?

Answering these questions will help you to realize how well you cope with stress, and how your coping mechanisms affect your relationships. The first chapter of this book is partly about helping you manage your stress; so, if you don't feel happy with any of these answers, return to Chapter One, and work through it until you feel more balanced and able to move on to this section. If you don't sort out the way in which you deal with stress, these problems will affect your relationships. Therefore, it's worth working at it because when you can stay calm and focused, you can enjoy so much more the benefits of a healthy relationship. If you're not in a relationship, it's worth dealing with this now so that there is less chance of this issue surfacing at a later date.

How to find the perfect partner

Many people think that relationship problems are inevitable, but many of these problems can be avoided by spending time working out what you want before you go into a relationship. The truth is that we'll never be perfect, so it's unlikely that we will be able to iron out all of our insecurities before we meet someone. We might be able to get rid of some of our insecurities, but when we get very close to people, our imperfections often become magnified. This section of the *Sort Your Life Out* programme is about ensuring that you're comfortable enough with yourself to get through the challenges that a relationship is likely to bring up.

So how do you know when you're ready for a relationship? People often look to meet someone: when other areas in their life are sorted; when many of their friends are married or in committed relationships; or, when they're simply weary of the singles' scene and tired of life alone. But none of these things necessarily means that you are ready for a relationship.

It can be hard to know when you are ready, willing *and* able to handle the commitment and challenges that a healthy, intimate relationship demands. So what do you need to have to be ready for true love? Well, one of the most important things is that you have to understand the expectations you have for relationships, as these will help you determine what kind of people you attract to you.

What are your relationship habits?

Whether you are currently out of a relationship and looking for one, in a relationship and happy, in a relationship and wanting to be *happier*, or trying to get out of one, this section will be really useful for you. It will give you the chance to step back and see how you tend to behave when you relate to other people.

I want you to do an exercise that will help you to identify the different kinds of relationships you have in your life and how you act in them. This will help you to develop a better understanding of your relationship habits.

Turn to a clean page in your *Sort Your Life Out* journal and list the ten most important relationships you have had in your life so far. These may include your partner, family, extended family, friends and work colleagues. You may even wish to include ex-partners and friends with whom you have lost touch, as these can also be a valuable source of information, particularly if they include long-term or significant relationships from the past.

Then I want you to write down the qualities and attributes that these people bring into the relationship, as well as the qualities and attributes that you bring. Break these down into both positive and negative qualities and attributes. In particular, when looking at past relationships, try to highlight what attributes made the relationship unworkable. Finally, note down all the positive and negative points about the relationship in general.

Your notes should look something like this:

Person	Positives	Negatives	What they do + −	What I do + −
Mum	Un-conditional	Take for granted	+ always there − nagging	+ caring − impatient
Husband	Mutual respect	Little time together	+ supportive − doesn't listen	+ patient − nagging

Looking over these notes, think about which of these relationships truly work and feel effortless. Which of these would you say require lots of effort and little reward – and which require little effort and lots of reward?

This exercise should start off the process of becoming aware of your relationship patterns. Now let's do something with this information.

Get protective

Any parent will tell you that when their child first starts playing with and making close friends with other children, they start to become protective, and worry about the influence that those friends have over their little babies. Many parents feel somewhat threatened, having worked hard to bring up children in a certain way that may, then, be undermined when other children and, indeed, adults, begin to influence them.

Now look back at the table you drew up in the last exercise, and consider yourself in the position of a protective parent. Look at each of the relationships in detail, and ask yourself this: if you were a protective parent, would you be happy for your child or children to be in each of these relationships? Which relationships would you be happy for them to continue? Which ones do you think are too negative?

Sometimes we have to step back and look at our situation as if we were looking at someone else. We rarely protect ourselves to the degree we should, so by pretending to be looking after one of the people closest to us, we can discover a different perspective.

Your relationship patterns

Many people think that the way we act in relationships is determined by our personality – something that can't be changed. In fact, some couples put up with arguments, incompatibilities and unnecessary nagging for years because they really don't believe that they can work these things out. I often see older couples settle into middle age and beyond with a resigned attitude to bickering. You hear people say things like 'she won't change now', 'that's just the way he is' or 'we've always been like this', and they fail to see that, with some work and attention, any of these patterns can change. The starting point for changing a pattern of behaviour – just like any other habit – is awareness.

What are your patterns?

To help yourself overcome a relationship pattern, you need to undo the months or years of practice that have built up, and then get to the root of the problem. As you work through this process of becoming aware of and then changing your habits, you'll gain some understanding of how your relationship patterns developed. You will also gain the strength to take ownership of those thoughts so that you can choose which ones you continue to have.

We find that we act and react in similar ways to similar situations time and time again, and, when repeated patterns are destructive, relationships can fall into a rut. For example, one lady I worked with had always been jealous of her partner's flirting. Right from the day they met, she hated the attention he gave to other women and felt very insecure about it. She would become moody with him, and when he found out why she was upset, rather than find a way to alleviate her anxieties, he felt trapped by her jealousy and so flirted more to prove to himself that he wasn't under her thumb. This made her even more jealous, which in turn made him feel more stifled. For ten years they both suffered because of this. They went up the same ladders every time they repaired the situation, and then back down the same snakes every time it happened again. I couldn't believe that two people could put up with such an obvious repeat pattern; but, like most people, they found it difficult to see what they were doing. They didn't understand that they could learn to react differently and that, with a bit of practice, they could both feel secure and comfortable.

This section of the programme will help you to identify

your own relationship habits, so that over 21 days you can start the process of re-learning how to behave. In doing so, you can enjoy relationships that are more loving and fun. In time, you can learn to see how others view the world so that you can accept their differences and even come to love them.

The past does not have to equal the future

Have you ever heard someone say, 'If I could just find the right person, everything would be all right'? Maybe you've even said this yourself. When someone says this, what they're usually saying is that they believe that *someone else* can make their life better. The truth is that we really need to work on ourselves first. Only we have the power to make our lives better.

As we become self-aware, we will find that we have to work on certain areas of our lives to banish bad habits, and replace them with healthy new ones. It is ultimately important to get closure on past issues, or you risk carrying them with you into present and future relationships, where they will be repeated. If you are confident that you've worked through your own personal issues in Chapter One of this book, you are probably ready to move on, particularly if you've mastered Chapter Three as well, which will ensure your confidence and self-esteem are at a good level.

Sometimes it takes a helping hand to move on from past relationships, and to uncover the negative patterns and habits that were either created or a feature of those relationships. Some people find that professional coaching or therapy can help them to move forward, and feel positive about finding and entering new relationships. If you think you need a little extra help, see page 177 for details. There is nothing wrong with accepting guidance from others, who are often in a position to see more clearly the problem behaviours that we carry with us. What is most important is that we learn to recognize and change them, which will prevent them from damaging future relationships in the same way.

Tools to find a perfect partner

Ticking the boxes

People often think that it's wrong to have a 'wish list' of things they are looking for in a partner, as it seems too rational or unromantic. But, whether or not we admit to having a 'wish list', it's normal and healthy to know the qualities we want in a partner. How else would we know we'd met someone we wanted to get close to?

So, here are some common characteristics that people often consider to be important in a partner. As you read down this list, consider how important each quality is for you, and then score it on a scale of 1 to 10 (with 1 being not at all important and 10 being very important). Write down your scores in your *Sort Your Life Out* journal, so that you can refer back.

- Good looking
- Funny
- Sensitive
- Affectionate
- Intelligent

- Adventurous
- Wealthy
- Sexy
- Great chemistry

It can be very easy to become swayed by chemistry when you first meet someone, and to be bowled over by dashing good looks or a charming personality. But the danger of being swept off your feet in this way is that you forget about some of the less obvious qualities that, further down the line, are critical to a happy relationship. So, while there's nothing wrong with finding someone attractive, when you know what you want and need from a future partner, you will be able to step back from the superficial things and take a view of whether this person has the deeper, longer-lasting characteristics and values that are important to you.

So here are some other things you may want to look for. A lot of these characteristics are things that are not necessarily apparent as soon as you meet someone, so I would also recommend that you take the time to get to know someone well before committing to them.

- I feel comfortable with this person and can be myself
- They listen to me and remember things I've said
- They don't put pressure on me to do or say things I'm not comfortable with
- I enjoy being in their company – and they in mine
- They don't try to manipulate and/or control me
- They are interested in my life – who I am, what I do, and what interests me, etc.
- They want me to be who I am and they don't want me

to change anything
- They want to be my friend as well as my lover
- We value similar things, such as family, honesty and friends
- We both have a say in any decisions, such as where to go on holiday and what to do at the weekend

As before, work down this list and think about which things are critical to you: write down the important things in your journal. When you meet someone and are in the head-over-heels stage when you may not find it easy to have a balanced perspective of the characteristics that are important to you in the long run, look back at these things to remind yourself of what you are looking for.

If you're in a relationship and you want to do this exercise, you could maybe discuss this with your partner, because it may help you both understand what it is you want from your relationship.

Step out of your comfort zone

I used to have a Comfort Zone where I knew I couldn't fail,
The same four walls of busy life were really more like jail.
I longed so much to do things I'd never done before,
But I stayed inside my Comfort Zone and paced the same old floor.
I said it didn't matter that I wasn't doing much,
I said I didn't care for things like hugs, kisses and such.

I claimed to be so busy with the things inside my Zone,
But deep inside I longed for someone special of my own.
I couldn't let my life go by, just watching others win.
I held my breath, stepped outside and let the change begin ...
I took a step and with new strength never felt before,
I kissed goodbye my Comfort Zone – and closed and locked
the door.

I was sent this verse some years ago by a lady who had read one of my books. She had been single for several years, and had believed she was doing everything in her power to meet someone. But, after stepping back from her life and looking at it from a fresh perspective, she realized that, although it seemed so obvious, she'd followed the same routine for years. She discovered that she'd failed to put herself in a position to experience new things, which included people. She used her routine as a comfort blanket to protect herself from her loneliness, and she was forced to come to terms with the fact that she couldn't rely on fate to throw Prince Charming in her path. She had to face her fears and do something different to increase her chances of meeting him.

Every time you step out of your comfort zone and do something different about meeting someone, put a coin in your *Sort Your Life Out* jar. This may include joining an Internet dating site, taking up a group activity that you haven't done before or going on a holiday for single people of your age. You may not have considered doing anything like this before, but take this opportunity to have some fun: the worst that could happen is that you try something different and make some new friends! At least you'll never have to wonder, what if...?

Tool 3:

Keep something for yourself

> *Relationships – of all kinds – are like sand held in your hand. Held loosely, with an open hand, the sand remains where it is. The minute you close your hand and squeeze tightly to hold on, the sand trickles through your fingers. You may hold onto some of it, but most will be spilled. A relationship is like that. Held loosely, with respect and freedom for the other person, it is likely to remain intact. But hold too tightly, too possessively, and the relationship slips away and is lost.*
>
> **Kaleel Jamison**

When we fall in love it can be so tempting to spend all of our time with our new partner; however, I strongly suggest that you make time for yourself. Do things for yourself that you enjoy, which could include going for a walk, playing sport, having a night out or a weekend away with other friends, or simply having a quiet night in on your own. Even if you feel that you want to see your 'new man' or 'woman' all the time, resist the urge to do everything with them. By retaining your independence you not only show them that you are not dependent upon them, but you do something for yourself as well. You'll be giving yourself the space to think about your needs and whether the relationship is meeting them.

With work, family and other personal commitments, I think it's realistic to schedule one weekly thing – something you do, just for you – that doesn't involve your partner. If you can and want to have more than one a week, that's great.

When you create some space for yourself, you keep a degree of perspective and you also maintain your own confidence without relying on someone else to make you feel good. We need to remember that relationships begin with ourselves. Therefore, the more we invest in ourselves, the happier we – and our relationships – will become. If we share our space with a partner who takes as much care of themselves as we do, the possibilities for happiness are endless.

Keep track of the 'dates' you have with yourself and put a coin in your *Sort Your Life Out* jar every time you make, and keep, a date with yourself.

How to make relationships work...

 Every good relationship, especially marriage, is based on respect. If it's not based on respect, nothing that appears to be good will last very long.
Amy Grant

Everyone who falls in love hopes that it will be forever. The truth is that relationships inevitably change, and few things in life cause more distress than the problems that develop when communication between partners breaks down. However, is it any wonder that so many relationships fail, considering the fact that we never really learn how to make a relationship work?

Believing that you will have nothing but successful

relationships in life is wholly misguided. It's a bit like buying a car, without knowing how to drive. You may get somewhere in it, but it will be more through luck than skill or judgement. We need to learn many things before we can 'drive' our relationships, and we need to take care of them, maintain them, if you like, much as we would a new car.

We need to work out why, after a period of time, we take our partners and relationships for granted, and why we show less respect and patience for one another. For a relationship to be successful, we need to learn how to keep the magic and excitement going, no matter what happens in life. As someone's faults appear and as challenges arise, rather than focus on these, we should focus on the positive elements to help the relationship grow and get stronger.

Let them be

Learning about your partner, learning how to let them be themselves, and learning how to compromise and share a space together is rarely going to be easy. You need to be able to talk, and you need to be prepared to face up to challenges when they arise. Many people, especially men, feel uncomfortable talking about their feelings, preferring to bottle things up than deal with what's really happening. The truth is that a successful relationship involves being honest with yourself, and honest with your partner. You need to see everything that is going on, rather than turning a blind eye. This is something that has been drummed into me from an early age by my parents, who have constantly reminded me about how hard they had to work at their marriage. Although it was tough, they stuck at it and to this day they continue to work hard and take life's ups and downs in their stride. They accept that it takes work and dedication to make a happy and healthy partnership – an attitude that many of us could benefit from.

What makes a good relationship?

From the earlier exercises, you will have a pretty good idea of how you act in relationships, the roles you play and the kind of problems you face. Awareness of what makes a good relationship and how we, as individuals, can contribute, not only helps to shape the nature of our future relationships, but may also take existing relationships to a higher level. It is true that most of the work involved in improving a relationship starts with the individual. If one person is clear and reasoned about what they want, and consistent about how they ask for it, the whole relationship can begin to take a new path. The following tools are all about you and your partner working together to have the best relationship possible.

 A relationship, I think, is like a shark, you know? It has to constantly move forward or it dies. And I think what we got on our hands is a dead shark.
Woody Allen

Tools to make a relationship work

I realize that in our hectic world, it can be hard to find time for your partner; however, if you're serious about working on your relationship, you need to make time once a week to prioritize your relationship, and spend some time discussing how you think things have been that week. You can talk about things that have niggled you as well as the good stuff – that way, you'll find out what you need less of, and what you need more of.

The most successful couples are those that make spending time together a priority. Like a plant without water, a relationship without time can wither and die. You need time to share your hopes and dreams, as well as your fears and failings, to keep in touch with what's happening in your lives, and to have fun.

See your relationship as a business

One of the things that makes it particularly challenging to work on improving a relationship is the lack of tangible ways to measure success and progress. Some people think it feels 'wrong' to treat an intimate relationship like a business, but there is some real benefit to this, especially from a male point of view. Perhaps if we viewed our relationships as business partnerships, where the management team have regular progress meetings, it would help resolve issues as they arise rather than letting resentment build – sometimes to the point where it's too overwhelming to tackle. Men often find it easier to express themselves when they're given structure and parameters, so some couples find it helpful to keep a regular check on their relationships by looking at what's going well and what isn't going so well.

Both you and your partner should answer the following questions:

- What's working and what makes me feel good?
- What doesn't make me feel good that I think could be improved?

Once you have your separate lists, you can compare them and discuss what each of you feels about the relationship. Spend time talking about why the positive things are so good; this will not only make you feel connected, but will also help you realize your strengths as a couple. Then move on to how you can improve the weaker areas.

Some of you may find it uncomfortable or unusual to look at your relationship in such a rational way; however, if you introduce and explain the concept to your partner, it can be a useful way to pinpoint some of the 'invisible' problems. For example, it may be easy to see that the socks on the floor drive you mad because socks are tangible things. It may not be so visible, however, that you are angry that your partner has stopped being loving and warm to you: so it can be helpful to have a structure that allows you to think about and highlight all the areas that could be improved. The aim is not to upset each other, but, rather, to explain why you feel that some areas need work, and to be specific about what needs improving. It's also a golden opportunity to celebrate the good points of your relationship, and to remind yourself of the things that make you want to work towards making it as good as it can be.

Resolving conflict in your relationships

The next two tools are about conflict. For relationships to survive in the modern world, both partners need to learn how to diffuse conflict and alleviate stress. It's inevitable that at some point you will have disagreements, and these will never be the 'end of the world'. Everyone gets angry, and does or says things they regret. Each of us deals with these types of issues in different ways. Some people shut down or withdraw, and some people like to attack the situation, and, in some cases, their partners, too.

Ironically, one of the main problems with conflict has nothing to do with conflict itself – it is the way people deal with it. Many people shy away from conflict; they think it's wrong, or they have no idea how to express themselves or positively address the situation in order to find solutions. One of the biggest hurdles many couples face is learning to change the way they habitually deal with conflict, and establish new, positive behaviours instead. We are all different. There will always be times when we disagree and when we upset other people. However, if we learn to deal with disagreements when they arise, we can move forward. If we fail to do so, each disagreement will feel like another dent in the relationship. After a few dents, resentment starts to seep in. It's far better to nip niggles in the bud before they grow out of proportion, and damage your relationship beyond repair.

You're stepping on my toe!

One of the most dangerous things one person can say to another is, 'the trouble with you is ...'. Why? Because the 'trouble' usually lies with the person who is making the observation. This is sometimes because the observer has let a niggle build up to the point where they can't take it any more.

I used to work with a couple who used to have massive

rows. The woman would regularly bring up things that had happened months ago, which bewildered her partner, who clearly had no recollection of saying or doing any of the things she mentioned. This woman expected her partner to understand, at all times, what he was doing to annoy her, when she had consistently failed to explain that she was upset, or why. He had always been much the same way, and she had lived with it for years without addressing the issues head on. I explained that it was like he had trodden on her toe, only to hear her cry 'ouch!' three months later.

When emotions like anger, frustration and resentment become a habit, they can seriously damage the love between two people. These emotions can, however, be avoided, if we deal with conflict at the time it occurs, and deal with it openly and honestly.

A key skill in dealing with conflict is learning to speak up about how you feel and what you think, and avoiding the temptation to sweep things under the carpet. This next tool is all about how to air your feelings in a calm, balanced and fair way.

The silent treatment

While men are often heard saying things like, 'she just goes on and on about things and it drives me mad', many women complain that 'he never wants to talk'. Well, both parties can be right! Although there are exceptions to the rule, men need to talk less than women, whereas women need to talk quite a lot. This exercise helps smooth communication because it limits the 'talking bit' to a period of time and it ensures that both sides have equal air time.

One partner speaks for five minutes. During this time the other partner listens and does not interrupt – at all! After all, 'silent' is an anagram of the word 'listen'. Men, in particular, appreciate the chance to have their say without interruption, as that is how they are used to talking with other men.

After this, the other person gets their say for five minutes.

After both of you have had an opportunity to speak, you will then give yourselves a further five minutes to discuss what has been said.

A few things to note: if you are talking about a major issue, you can obviously talk for longer than five minutes. And, similarly, if it is about a small niggle or point, you don't have to speak for the full five minutes. However, be aware that people who don't feel comfortable sharing how they feel may well say, after one minute, 'That's me done. I don't have anything else to say.' In this case, as the listener, sit in silence and wait to see what else comes up. Something invariably will.

Stop the blame game

When you argue or when something goes wrong in your relationship, do you ask who is at fault or who is to blame? Sadly, this is what many people do, and it is the path to no resolution! What does work much more effectively is for both partners to accept that they share joint responsibility for the relationship and its problems – and that they should work together to solve them.

So, for the next 21 days, whenever something goes wrong in your relationship, rather than pointing the finger of blame at your partner (or unnecessarily carrying the blame yourself) try to see what it is about the way in which you and your partner work together that has led to the problem.

One way in which to broach tricky subjects is to use a four-step tactic:

1. State the situation in a factual way
2. Explain how you interpret it
3. Explain how it makes you feel
4. State the consequences of that

For example, if your partner, who is usually chatty with you, comes home and is silent all evening, you might say:

1. I've noticed you haven't said much tonight
2. This makes me think that something is wrong
3. Because you're not talking, I feel a little rejected
4. And I'm worried that this is a sign that there is something wrong with our relationship

The benefit of this technique is that you are factual where you can be; however where there are feelings involved, you take ownership for them, rather than blaming your partner for making you feel a particular way.

When you use this tool, you will learn to see how honesty and awareness can help you experience a new depth of understanding and trust, rather than feeling like a situation is out of your control.

Have some fun

Humour and playfulness are shared pleasures that create a sense of intimacy and connection – two of the healthiest qualities that a relationship can have. Humour can add life not only to your intimate relationship but also all the relationships you share. Humour adds a sense of spontaneity, helping us to let go of defensiveness by lowering everyone's defences, helping us to release inhibitions, and making it easier to express our emotions openly.

Try to have fun like you did when you were first together. If you can't remember what that felt like, look at a new couple and notice how light they are together. There is no reason why you can't be like that again. If you're having problems, it really helps if you and your partner take time out to do something playful together; for example, playing a sport or seeing a silly movie. Then, come back to discussing your problems, and you are more likely to have a new perspective on things.

How to know when it's time to end a relationship

Relationships can be a great source of love, pleasure, support and excitement. However, sad though it may be, if they go wrong, they can also be a source of grief and anguish.

There can be many reasons for wanting to get out of a relationship. Some of these include, quite simply, not wanting to be with that person, or discovering that after the initial period of being in love, you no longer feel any love for them at all. Another common reason for relationships coming to an end occurs when you and your partner have reached a stage of life where you both want incompatible things, and you can't find a compromise. For example, you can't agree on whether to have children or about where you want to live.

While these are common reasons for many people, others find they need to leave a relationship because it is abusive. The first step to leaving a relationship is admitting there is something wrong between you and your significant other.

Warning signs

Many people worry or become frightened about leaving or upsetting a partner, especially if they are afraid of them. However, ironically, the longer they stay together, the more likely it is that the relationship will become dysfunctional. In these cases there are some very clear warning signs that the relationship has become abusive, and that leaving should be seriously considered. Some common signs are:

- Your partner tries to control you, and exercise power over you
- Your partner gives you verbal insults and nasty putdowns
- You feel suffocated and trapped
- Your partner is abusive to you either physically, mentally, sexually, or all of these

While there are numerous reasons why people don't leave (for example, joint finances, children or the hope that things will just get better), in situations like these, many people stay put because they don't have the self-esteem and confidence to leave; they may also be very afraid of what their partner will do if they walk away.

Even though there are two of you involved, when it comes to thinking about the future of your relationship, I strongly suggest you put yourself first, and think long and hard about your long-term happiness. Consider what it would be like to stay with your partner for both a few months' and a few years' time. How does that thought make you feel? By thinking about a potential future with your current partner, you will get a sense of whether you feel hopeful that things can be sorted out or whether you dread the thought of more time spent being unhappy. While we have no way of predicting the future, this simple exercise can tell you more about your current state of mind.

Be honest with yourself. Breaking up is rarely an easy option, but if you have strong reasons and feelings that you want to leave a relationship, then have the courage of your convictions and do what is necessary. Often the person instigating the break feels guilty when they see that their partner is in pain, and may be tempted to stay. If this is the case, you are not doing yourself or your partner any favours. By staying, you are preventing both of you from being free to find someone who truly appreciates and wants to be with you. So, if you're finding it particularly hard to leave, tell friends about what you are doing and ask them for their support – both emotional and practical – where necessary. Having people around you who care can really help you, and there may be practical ways that they can help: for example, you may find that you are more likely to leave a relationship if you know that you have somewhere to stay in the short term.

If you think you may be in an unhealthy relationship, read through the following statements. If you can relate to any or all of them, you may be staying in your relationship for the wrong reasons:

- I think I'll never meet someone new
- I think it's better to put up with what I've got
- I believe that anything is better than being alone
- I deserve this relationship
- He/she will change if I'm patient; he/she is really a good person
- He/she really needs me, he/she just doesn't realize it
- I'm nothing without my partner and/or our relationship

By reading through this list, and possibly relating to some of these things, you may realize that they are not necessarily good reasons to stay in a relationship. If you read these statements and don't relate to any of them, and you and your partner both feel that you have a happy future together, then this gives you a good indication that you have a strong foundation.

Whether you want to leave a relationship or work on the one you're in, there are a number of great organizations that offer support and counselling to those with relationship difficulties: one of the best known is Relate (www.relate.org. uk). Relate do see people on their own, but the focus of their work is with couples. If you would prefer to speak privately to someone about relationships or other issues, you can contact the British Association of Counsellors and Psychotherapists www.bacp.co.uk) or your GP may be able to refer you. By speaking to a qualified therapist or counsellor, you may find that you look at your relationship from a different perspective and so are able to gain clarity on the right thing for you, whether that be to end your relationship or to work through your problems.

The most important relationship of all

Relationships are essential for life because we are naturally social beings. It's important that we engage in relationships in which we not only give to others, but in which we receive nourishment from other people, which, in turn helps us to feel good about ourselves. I know this might sound a bit fluffy, but the heart of any relationship lies in the relationship we have with ourselves. If that relationship is a strong one, we can get so much more out of life and all there is to enjoy in the world, by simply loving and appreciating who we are.

Sort Your Life Out journal

DAY:

TOOLS I'M USING TODAY:

-
-
-
-
-

THOUGHTS, FEELINGS AND OBSERVATIONS:

-
-
-
-
-

3 POSITIVE THINGS THAT HAPPENED TODAY:

-
-
-

ANY OTHER NOTES E.G. FOOD/ACTIVITY DIARY:

5

SORT YOUR LIFE OUT:
Happiness

The purpose of our lives is to be happy.
The 14th Dalai Lama

There once was a small village in the centre of India that was said to suffer from a strange disease called laziness. An American heard of this rare disease and set off to find this village, and to cure them of their ailment. After several days of travelling, he entered the village and it wasn't long before he came across a middle-aged man lying in a hammock. The man was sipping a drink with a contented smile on his face. Delighted to find a specimen of laziness so quickly, the American waved his hand in front of the man's face and asked him what he was doing.

'I am lying in a hammock,' replied the man.

'Yes, but what do you do for a living?' asked the American.

'I fish,' came the reply.

'Have you caught any fish today?'

'Yes, I caught two big ones this morning.'

'Then why don't you go and fish more?' enquired the American.

'What for?' asked the man.

'Well, because then you could sell your surplus fish at the market and buy a fishing boat, which would enable you to catch even more fish.'

'What for?' asked the man again.

'Well, with the profits from that, you would be able to afford a trawler, and then you could catch so many fish that you would be able to sell to the neighbouring villages as well.'

'What for?' repeated the man.

'Well, with the profits from that, you could build a bigger house, a gazebo and a swimming pool, and you could buy an expensive car to travel whenever and wherever you please.'

'What for?' repeated the man.

'Well, to be happy, of course!' snapped the American, losing his patience.

'I am happy already,' the man responded. 'Why go to all that effort for something I already have?'

All of us want to be happy, and we spend a lot of time and energy doing things that we think will make us happier. But, is it possible that – like the man in the story – we *already* have all the ingredients we need to be happy? The purpose of this part of the *Sort Your Life Out* programme is to help you explore what you can do to become happier in all areas of your life. So, before we go any further, let's make sure we're talking about the same thing.

What is happiness?

In this section of the book, I am inviting you to look at happiness and become curious about how to get it. It may well be that you've been looking for it in the wrong place. In helping you to sort your life out, my dream is that you become happy for no reason at all, and that you learn to be happy with what you've already got. Happiness is what we're searching for and yet, as I sit down to write this chapter, it seems to be the hardest thing to define. What makes me happy today may not make me happy tomorrow, and what makes *me* happy is not necessarily the same thing that makes *you* happy. For example, when I was growing up, happiness, apparently, was a cigar called Hamlet, or so the advertisers led us to believe. How ironic, given what we now know about the dangers of smoking!

We always have to be careful when we use a word as a label to describe a complex emotion. However, for the purpose of this book, I am going to try and define what I mean by happiness. I believe that happiness is a general state of positive emotion that has an underlying sense of purpose and meaning. Hopefully that strikes a chord with you. In terms of this definition, how can you tell whether or not you're happy?

This question suggests that happiness is an on/off state – you either have happiness or you don't. It also suggests that if you manage to attain happiness, you can hang on to it like you would any other possession.

The truth is, however, that happiness, as most of us know it, is not a destination or a solid state – it changes and moves, and it enters and leaves our lives for different reasons. Happiness can evolve and change so constantly that the goal posts for achieving it move as well. However, instead of beginning an unproductive search for an elusive 'something' that changes so often, why not simply *do* more of the things that make us happy, and acknowledge the things in our lives that *already* make us happy.

What makes you smile?

We often say that we should 'count our blessings', but how many of us actually take time out to do this? The phrase has become something of a cliché, but that's probably because it's true. Before I tell you about how you can become happier, let's look at all the things you have in your life right now that bring you joy.

Take a clean page in your *Sort Your Life Out* journal, and write a list of everything in your life for which you are grateful. Here are some ideas:

- A supportive loving partner
- Beautiful children
- A clean bill of health
- A secure home
- Friends on whom I can rely
- My dog/cat/rabbit, etc.
- My sense of humour
- My community
- Someone to hug in the morning
- Clean water, warmth, shelter, etc.
- A flexible job
- One lovely holiday each year

You can also write down the little things that make you smile, even if they seem insignificant or immaterial. These could include something you own, like your car or an item of clothing, a song or album of music that you love, a hobby that helps you to relax, or a favourite film or television show that is guaranteed to make you feel good.

While our happiness levels go up and down depending on what is going on in our lives, I want you to realize that happiness is comprised of both big and small things. We most commonly think about happiness being an intangible quality, but this quick exercise has hopefully helped you to focus on the things you already have that make you happy. I'm now going to share with you another way of assessing your happiness.

The Happiness Equation

A few years ago, I conducted a piece of research about happiness, with Dr Carol Rothwell, a clinical psychologist. It was called 'The Happiness Equation', and we found that by answering some questions and doing a simple calculation, you can, in fact, score your overall levels of happiness. But, before you get a chance to do the equation yourself, here are the main findings of the research we did.

We found that, with the exception of people who don't have enough financial security to live comfortably, and despite huge rises in wealth and consumer power relative to previous decades, people don't experience significant shifts in levels of happiness. We appear to overemphasize the perceived long-term benefits of quick-hit factors (such as winning the lottery), but also tend to believe that sudden, dramatic negative events (for example, loss of mobility, sight or hearing) will have a lasting impact on our overall happiness. However, just as the effect of dramatic positive events is short-lived, research consistently shows that although they do experience a short-term drop in wellbeing, people who have experienced some traumatic event soon return to a similar level of happiness as they had before.

So it seems that long-term happiness must therefore be something more than just a response to immediate environmental factors and quick fixes. Here's what we found them to be.

What affects our happiness?

Critical factors in defining levels of national happiness are: the absence of sufficient resources to provide basic food, shelter and clothing; social and racial inequality; political unrest; and poor access to a meaningful education. However, simply having these things is not, in itself, a guarantee of happiness. With our basic needs met, we can then enjoy social, spiritual and economic things that affect our levels of happiness. We can simplify these ideas by thinking about happiness in terms of three fundamental areas, which make up the Happiness Equation.

Personal characteristics: We all have personal characteristics, which in part define how we relate to other people, face challenges and adapt to changes in life. People who are outgoing, energetic, optimistic, resilient and flexible will also tend to be happier. It seems that some of these characteristics are inherited and some can be learned – which also means they can be unlearned. Our research suggests that this accounts for approximately 20 per cent of our overall levels of happiness.

Existence needs: As we found at a national level, individuals need to have met a range of basic existence needs before they are able to experience happiness to any significant degree. The most important of these basic needs include health, financial security, personal safety, a sense of belonging and engaging in meaningful activities. As I've already said, not having these affects our ability to survive but not necessarily our ability to be happy. In the USA, for example, it has been found that billionaires see themselves as only slightly happier than people with average incomes.

Higher order needs: Finally, there are a number of higher-order happiness factors that relate to a deeper outlook on life and personal relationships. These include self-esteem, challenge, meeting expectations, depth of relationships and intensity of experience.

Put together, these three components can be used to gauge our overall level of happiness. They can also help to pinpoint the things we need to work on to become happier.

How to calculate happiness

Now is your chance to see how these factors are affecting your level of happiness. There are four questions to the Happiness Equation: the first two relate to personal characteristics; the third to unhappiness factors; and the fourth to happiness factors. To find out how happy you are, read each of the four statements and circle the number on the scale that you feel reflects most accurately where you are at the moment in your life. Enter the four ratings into the equation and complete the

calculation. If you want to do this online, visit http://www.
sortyourlifeout.com/book. By filling in these questions online,
the system will work out your happiness score for you.

1 *Personal traits:* To what extent do you see yourself as
someone who is outgoing, energetic, flexible and open to
change?

To a large extent										Not at all
10	9	8	7	6	5	4	3	2	1	0

2 *Outlook on life:* To what extent do you see yourself as
someone who takes a positive outlook on life, bounces back
quickly from setbacks, feels that you, and not fate, is driving
your life?

To a large extent										Not at all
10	9	8	7	6	5	4	3	2	1	0

3 *Basic existence needs:* To what extent do you feel your basic
needs in life are met in relation to personal health, financial
subsistence, personal safety, freedom of choice, sense of
community/belonging and access to education/knowledge?

Definitely met										Definitely not met
10	9	8	7	6	5	4	3	2	1	0

■ *Higher-order happiness needs:* To what extent are you currently able to...
■ Call on the support of people close to you
■ Immerse yourself in what you're doing
■ Meet your expectations
■ Engage in meaningful activities that give you a sense of purpose
■ Feel a clear sense of who you are and what you're about

Give yourself one score out of 10 for your overall higher-order happiness needs.

Completely										Not at all
10	9	8	7	6	5	4	3	2	1	0

WORKING OUT YOUR HAPPINESS QUOTIENT

Happiness = Personal Traits + Outlook + (5 x Existence Needs) + (3 x Higher-order Needs)

Your Score:
Happiness = _____ + _____ + (5 x _____) + (3 x _____)
Happiness = _____/100

WHAT DOES YOUR SCORE MEAN?

When this work was first published, it was broadcast in 27 countries worldwide. Some people thought that we had found the definitive answer to happiness. Some journalists from Korea even flew over to the UK to interview us in person. But we don't have the perfect answer, and you might even think that it seems a little strange to say, for example, that someone is 48 per cent happy, as happiness is relative. It's not about comparing your score to someone else's; instead, you can use this equation at different times to see how your life has changed. You can use your current score as a starting point from which to become happier – and you may even want to check it again in 21 days, or at regular intervals, after you've been using the tools at the end of the section.

Happiness through the life cycle

A recent study on happiness[4] found that people are happiest at the beginning and the end of their lives. This U-shaped curve of happiness was discovered by examining social survey data from 500,000 people across Europe and the USA. After controlling for other factors that affect happiness, such as divorce, job loss and level of income, the average low point of happiness fell somewhere between the ages of 40 and 50, with men and women in the UK being most unhappy when they were 44.

At the beginning of life, we tend to be excited about every day that dawns. At the end of life, people tend to be glad to be alive because they realize how precious and fragile it is. It's the chunk of time in between these stages when we often take for granted the fact we're alive; and, instead of appreciating what we have, we get lost in meeting the demands of everyday life.

 We do not remember days, we remember moments.
Cesare Pavese

This curve of pleasure throughout life is similar to that which we experience when we're on holiday. At the start of a holiday most people are so excited about being away that they really enjoy themselves, and, similarly, in the last few days, as the return home looms large, people tend to make the most of their time away because they know it's coming to an end. But the days in the middle often get lost and less appreciated.

The scientists involved in this research were puzzled by these findings, and you may well be surprised, too. For me, this study simply confirmed what I have seen happening in the lives of my own clients. For years now, I've seen so many people seek out life coaching during what some might call 'mid-life', because they reach a point where they supposedly have everything they need to be happy – and yet they're not. I've also seen people reach this stage of disillusionment earlier and earlier. A crisis is no longer just something that happens in middle age. With the pressures of modern-day life starting in our twenties, I'm seeing younger and younger people, particularly men, looking for answers. And many of them ask the question, 'is this all there is?' They have all the things that they thought would make them happy, and yet they still feel as if something is missing.

I'm having a mid-life crisis

I was recently asked to be a spokesman for a study that was commissioned by Norwich Union,[5] the UK's largest life insurance company. The study did, in fact, find that the low point of life, often known as a mid-life crisis, is happening even

earlier nowadays for men. Some 71 per cent of the men sur-
veyed, who were in their thirties, claimed that they were
experiencing or had experienced a so-called 'Bloke Break-
down' and over one-third said they had seen a friend or colleague go through a mid-life crisis. Reasons for a crisis included comparing themselves to friends on career achievements,
looks, financial worries and relationship difficulties. It was
also found that, rather than sports cars and gadgets being the
signs of a crisis, you can tell if a man is at a low point if he
takes a career sabbatical (56 per cent), takes up yoga (39 per
cent) or turns to self-help books for guidance (35 per cent).

These are not negative things in themselves; rather, they
demonstrate that men have reached a point in life where they
are looking for something external to make them happier.
Women don't escape lightly, either. It was found that women
still feel more pressure to look younger than men (78 per cent
versus 57 per cent). What all of this tells me is that people
are looking for answers and enlightenment – they want to
know how to be happy. Some of these answers are buried in
the teachings of scholars and wise people from thousands of
years ago; so let's take a look at what they had to say.

The history of happiness

Being present

I find it amazing that as far back as 2,300 years ago, people
like Mencius (a philosopher who lived during the period of the
Chinese Warring States; 370–286 BCE), believed that the more
joy we find in the process of doing things, the more moti-

vated we are. He believed that this, in turn, led us to grow. So whether they were washing clothes, cooking meals, talking to a neighbour or harvesting rice, people could find happiness simply in the doing of things. Not everything had to have a purpose or a reason other than it needed to be done and by not rushing these tasks, people were able to lose themselves in the simplicity of life. This is something we are far removed from because nowadays we tell ourselves that everything has to be done for a reason or to reach a goal.

You're having a laugh

Zhuangzi, a Chinese philosopher who lived at a similar time as Mencius (the 4th century BCE), claimed that a sense of humour was critical to happiness. He believed that when we laugh, we stop being rational, and that by freeing ourselves from rational thought, we can just go along with things as they are, rather than feeling pressure to do or have more. He would have found it hilarious to see how seriously we live our lives today, and how we run around in such a frenzy seeking out profit – both monetary and personal – wherever we can. It's sad but true that many adults lack humour in their own behaviour, and take themselves far too seriously.

Crave on

Similarly, Buddha, who many people think of as the greatest philosopher who ever lived, believed that the cause of unhappiness is 'craving' (or, as he called it 'mental dysfunction' or 'dukkha'). This is true for so many of us today, because we crave ever more money, beauty, possessions, attention, love, and so on. Craving comes from the belief that we don't have enough of something, or that we are lacking in something that would bring us more happiness. For example, we may aspire to have more money because this would afford us a bigger house and that, in turn, would make our quality of life significantly better; or we may want to lose weight because we believe that by having the perfect figure, our problems will go away. The last of the ancient philosophers, Aristotle, who was living on the other side of the world in Greece, in the 4th century BCE, had a similar view of happiness. He said that we had to depend on ourselves for happiness, rather than look to satisfy our cravings to make us happy.

Selling yourself short

In the 1940s, psychologist Abraham Maslow also looked at what made people fulfilled and happy. He concluded that, 'the story of the human race is the story of men and women selling themselves short' and he believed that in order to reach the highest levels of fulfilment and happiness, we had to have first of all met our basic needs. These things include having food, clothing, shelter and security. After these basic needs, we seek to gain love and recognition from others and then only once these are in place can we be creative and discover how to express ourselves to find true happiness.

Scoring goals

Austrian neurologist, psychiatrist and Holocaust survivor Viktor Frankl said that, rather than put ourselves under stress to achieve goals, humans need to strive for a goal that has some meaning for them. This idea came from his own experience of surviving the Holocaust, which he wrote about in his famous book, *Man's Search for Meaning*. Tragic as the Holocaust was, Frankl was able to find personal meaning in the experience, which provided him with the will to survive it. Frankl also found research that showed a strong relationship between 'meaninglessness' and criminal behaviours, addictions and depression; he believed that without meaning, people filled the void in their life with hedonistic pleasures, cravings for power, materialism, hatred, boredom or neurotic obsessions and compulsions. While you don't have to have had such a traumatic survival experience in your life to find meaning, Frankl's point about having a sense of purpose relates to happiness because happy people are often ones who find joy and meaning in doing the simplest of things.

Making others happy

Most recently, a new branch of psychology has emerged, which focuses on the study of happiness. Martin Seligman, one of the pioneers of Positive Psychology, a school of psychology that looks at happiness and wellbeing, says that one of the best ways to discover happiness is by nourishing our unique strengths in contributing to the happiness of other people. By striving towards a purpose greater than ourselves, and helping other people, we experience a deep sense of fulfilment.

Hang out with your friends

Finally, Ed Diener, the other pioneer of Positive Psychology, concludes that happiness is important because it is the foundation of success in many other areas of life, such as careers, relationships and physical health. Diener also believes that tragic events only lead to temporary unhappiness – from which truly happy people tend to bounce back. I take this to mean that rather than find reasons not to be happy because of what may not be working in our life, we gain more happiness by looking for ways in which we can work towards the positive.

When I was looking back over the history of happiness, I realized that it is important for us to pause for a moment and consider the truth in what these people are saying. Later on in this chapter, you'll see that some of the tools you'll be practising for 21 days reflect these key points.

Getting in our own way

Yesterday, when I was taking a break from writing this book, I chatted to a friend of mine on the phone. As happiness was on my mind, I asked him what made him happy. He paused for a moment and then said, 'Nobody's ever asked me that before.' This got me thinking.

As you already know, when I was very young, I was very happy in my own little world. But, as I got older, I became more insecure and wanted to fit into the world around me to be happy. I wanted to have what my friends had – the same remote-controlled car and the same clothes – and I wanted to listen to the same music. Then, when I reached adulthood, I received the message that I needed to make money, get married, have children and then live happily ever after. There was always something else to have and work towards and do, as I moved through the next stage of life. There never seemed to be a point where I could just sit back and enjoy what I already had.

Many people never stop to think about what makes them happy; in fact, it seems that most people blindly follow the formula to which they were exposed at a young age. For many people living in this modern world, happiness is a destination that we never seem to reach. It's always just around the corner, because there's always something else to do or have before we reach that elusive goal. The world tells us that we cannot be happy as we are, because we need A, B and C to be good enough. Then, after getting A, B and C, we usually want D, E and F, to get to the next stage of happiness. And so on. However, there are some people who never achieve A, B and C, and are left feeling inadequate and unhappy with their lot. And, ironically, a lot of people who achieve all of these things (which include wealth, success and material possessions) still find that they're not happy.

But has it always been this way? Let's explore how you find happiness in your day-to-day life. Some of the things that make you happy will be things that society dictates; however, there will be other experiences that I want you to think about by answering the following questions. I suggest you write these down in your journal.

- What makes you happy?
- What have been some of the happiest moments of your life so far?
- What made you happy when you were a child?
- What do you think would make you happy in the future?

Take some time over the next few days or even weeks to

explore these answers further. Why not keep these questions tucked in the front of your journal, and look at them regularly, adding things to the lists as you become more aware of things that bring you happiness. By knowing what gives you joy at a deep level, you will start to shift your awareness from external definitions of happiness to the ones that are personal to you.

 The foolish man seeks happiness in the distance, the wise man grows it under his feet.
James Openhelm

Synthetic versus natural happiness

Ultimately possessions and experiences give us a synthetic kind of happiness; what we should really be aiming for is a natural type of happiness that comes from a place inside ourselves. To some degree, this comes from two things: having a sense of purpose about our own happiness and the positive feelings we get from helping others.

So, firstly, when it comes to meaning and purpose I am not here to tell you what yours should be; however, I have found, through my own personal explorations and my work with many people, that the happiest people are the ones who find their purpose and meaning in overcoming their imperfections and insecurities. Once we accept that we already have what we need to be happy we can start to enjoy our imperfections and rise above them. This allows us to see that we are more than the sum of our experiences to date and that we always have a choice about how we feel and act. We also have a choice about what we can go on to experience: our past does not have to repeat itself. This phenomenon has even been researched by scientists. Dr Gregory Berns of Emory University in the USA has found that the key to enjoying sustained satisfaction is to make an effort to do and try new things, and also to be motivated about and committed to doing something that has personal significance.[6] It's in this kind of open attitude that some people are able to find purpose in pursuing their own happiness.

Secondly, in looking at helping others, I have daily direct experience of how this brings me happiness. My life has a meaning and purpose through my work and that is a by-product of me looking after myself and enjoying my life, and what I do: because I look after my own wellbeing and happiness, I have enough spare energy to expend on working with those who need help. I would not be able to do a good job with other people if I was run down or unhappy in my own life. If I feel good, then chances are those with whom I work will too, because I carry that positive feeling into my work.

These two elements of natural happiness – having a sense of purpose about our own happiness and helping others – are not the most obvious causes of happiness for most people. Most of us, if we think about what makes us happy, will often think of things that make up synthetic happiness.

Does money make us happy?

One of the things that we tend to think adds to our happiness levels is money. So, does money make the world go round? Well, actually it does. Not only are we told that we need to have a certain lifestyle, we are also given the message that to be happy we need to have the right car, phone, clothes, hairstyle, holidays and so on. Most of these things rely on us having money. Money buys you all of the 'stuff' that makes you happy, so it's easy to believe that money is the answer to happiness – but it is synthetic happiness. The truth is, though, that there are many people with lots of money who are far from happy.

According to Peter Ubel, a professor of medicine at the University of Michigan,[7] there is very little correlation between money and happiness. In various surveys it has been found that wealth only accounts for 1 per cent of happiness. It's true that for some people the correlation is higher, but this tends to be people who are very poor and for whom an increase in income makes a significant difference to their basic quality of life. For those of us who already have our basic needs met, which is the majority of us who have food, shelter and clothing, getting more money does not lead to more happiness – we just believe it does. So, it seems that once we have reached a level of income whereby we meet our fundamental survival needs, any money over and above this only adds to our synthetic happiness; we need to look to non-financial things to experience true natural happiness.

What would you do if you won the lottery?

How many times have you asked or been asked this question? I know this is a fairly common topic of conversation around a dinner table or around the watercooler on a dull Wednesday afternoon. People tend to say things like 'I'd give up my job', 'I'd pay off my mortgage' or 'I'd buy a yacht/sportscar/ holiday home'. Well, once you've done all of that, what would you do then?

In our work on the equation to calculate happiness, Dr Carol Rothwell and I interviewed ten lottery winners. What we found was that, in spite of their wealth, most of these people were no happier than anyone else. In fact, some of these people wished they'd never won the lottery at all. Some of them were bankrupt; some had so much money that they were overwhelmed and had no idea what to do with it; and all of them had suffered from pestering not only by friends and family, but also by charities and organizations asking for donations. They felt guilty for having a lot of money, but not enough money to give to everyone, and so they didn't know where to donate. They had no need to get up in the morning, other than to spend money, so their lives started to lack meaning and purpose. The exception was one man who gave away all of his winnings to worthy causes. He kept nothing for himself, his life carried on as it had before, and he was happier for having helped others.

Why doesn't wealth make us happy?

 Nowadays people know the price of everything and the value of nothing.
Oscar Wilde

It has been found that being rich does not make us consistently happy because most of us don't know what to do with large sums of money. A lot of us assume that just having lots of zeros at the end of our bank balance will automatically make us feel happier. But if I were to give you £1 million in cash right now, how would you feel? Imagine holding that money in your hands. What would you do with it?

Just by having £1 million more than you currently have, you would not have changed. What makes the difference to the way you feel is what you do with the money you have. Very few people give enough thought to what they would spend the money on, how it would make them feel and the responsibility that comes with having wealth. George Loewenstein, economist at Carnegie Mellon University, found that we overestimate the amount of long-term pleasure that money brings and that in order to be happy even after earning, winning or inheriting substantial amounts of money, we either need to spend some of it on worthwhile causes or we need to see it simply as money, rather than as the solution to any problems we may have.

The price of happiness

One woman came to see me because she wanted to curb her spending. She got a massive jolt of happiness from buying things, and her house was filled with stuff. She had four credit cards maxed out, yet she was still compulsively spending. Her real weakness was shoes. I remember standing in her bedroom and asking her to take all of her shoes out of the wardrobe. The bed, the floor and every available space was soon covered in shoes, and she didn't even remember buying some of them. I asked her how many of those pairs of shoes were making her happy at that moment. Given that she was far from happy in her life, she replied that although some of them were lovely and still made her smile, on the whole her shoe habit had only brought her misery. Buying the shoes had brought temporary happiness, but once the thrill of a new pair of heels had worn off, she needed to buy another pair to feel good again.

This lady was running on what is known as the 'hedonic treadmill'. In a nutshell, this means that we constantly adapt or become used to having better and more things, so that they no longer provide us with positive emotions. We need more and more, and bigger and better, to get the same thrills, which keeps us on the treadmill indefinitely.

So, when we are on the hedonic treadmill, the more we have, the more we need to boost our happiness – and that's when the pursuit of happiness becomes exhausting. Psychological research has shown that as we become wealthier, we adjust our expectations. What we aspired to yesterday becomes today's new baseline. This adaptation means that it will take a further hike in wealth for us to get the same rush of happiness, even though in relation to previous earnings we may be considerably richer. Society has led us to believe so many things about money, however, hopefully by reading this section, you will realize that by focusing on and continually striving towards a future state, we can never be satisfied or happy. The rest of this chapter and the tools that follow will give you the chance to work out what specifically makes you happy.

 When you can't have what you want, it's time to start wanting what you have.
Kathleen A. Sutton

Living in a pressure cooker

The modern world is full of stress, without the extra pressure of needing material things to keep up with other people. When material goods are surplus to what we need (i.e., simply what we 'want') they only bring us a synthetic kind of happiness. By buying into the need to have them, we further increase the amount of pressure we're under, until life becomes very challenging.

If you look back through time, life was much simpler. Although there was less 'luxury' around, there was also less pressure to conform, and people gained pleasure from simpler things. This pressure to conform has increased a great deal in the last 50 years, and one of the areas where the impact has been the most profound involves the way we look. What I'm going to suggest you do is step back from the need to conform for a while and, by taking a different perspective on the way you look, you will find you are not getting as involved in these pressures. I will be helping you to look at what *really* makes you happy, and what makes you happy temporarily, conditionally or synthetically.

You can be happy just as you are...

If you watch adverts on television or at the cinema, or if you look at advertisements on the side of buses and on billboards, you could come away thinking that you are rather inadequate if you don't have the right lifestyle. But you don't need any of this stuff. The latest handbag does not make you a good person. And the most up-to-date mobile phone does not make you confident. To feel truly happy, you need to accept who you are. Regardless of what you do for a living, where you live, how much money you have, and what you look like, the real you is the same – and that is the part of you that can experience natural happiness.

Tools for happiness

The fundamental principle of Positive Psychology, or the so-called 'Science of Happiness', as I mentioned earlier, is the idea that we can improve our wellbeing and happiness by adopting certain habits and attitudes usually found in happy and optimistic people. This concept is reflected in this part of the programme, where I will be challenging you to go out there and explore what it takes for you to get happy. Because this is a relatively new area, who knows how much you can change your happiness levels in 21 days? But by using the following tools, I'd like you to find out what you can achieve in this time and how much difference you can make …

Here's the present

First I was dying to finish high school and start college
*   and then*
I was dying to finish college and start working and then
I was dying to marry and have children and then
I was dying for my children to grow old enough for school
*   so I could return to work and then*
I was dying to retire

And now
I am dying and suddenly I realize that I forgot to live
Dr Wayne Dyer

When was the last time you did something and gave it 100 per cent of your attention? We have become so preoccupied by adding days to our lives, we are in danger of forgetting to add life to our days. By trying to cram as much as we can into our busy lives, we dilute the benefits and can end up dissatisfied or nonplussed by life. If we can become more conscious in every moment, and learn to focus on just one thing at a time, rather than juggling several things, not paying any real attention to the task in hand, we may well get greater satisfaction and happiness from the simpler things. Young children do this effortlessly; they have no concept of yesterday or tomorrow. Sadly, however, as we grow older, most of us develop the habit of thinking too much and not enjoying where we are now.

Many people spend a lot of their lives trying to achieve goals. In most cases, a goal is merely a stepping-stone to another goal, which is in turn a stepping-stone to something else. There isn't necessarily anything wrong with this, but for one thing the pleasure of achieving a goal is diminished when we move so quickly on to the next goal. Furthermore, we can become obsessed with goals, never stopping to enjoy the here and now. I have met many, many people who are so goal-focused and spend so much time thinking ahead that they are missing out on the happiness that can be gained from the simple pleasure of enjoying what's happening in the present.

Some of the most successful and happy people I have met

are brilliant at shutting up the Duck in their heads. They are able to immerse themselves totally in what they are doing at any given moment, and spend relatively little time mulling over the past or projecting into the future. This skill of being present is something that is absolutely critical for top sportspeople. I have been fortunate enough to work with many sporting champions and most of them realize the value of this. They spend a lot of time practising being present, not only to achieve happiness, but to be more successful at their game. The way that I help them is by teaching them how to block off inward distractions by remembering times when they were totally present.

Just take a minute now to remember some of the greatest moments in your life. Everybody has times when they where completely immersed in something – watching the sun set on a beautiful day, walking barefoot on a beach, or smiling or hugging someone they love.

So, over the next 21 days, challenge yourself to spend as much time as you can being present. If you notice yourself worrying or getting stressed, I want you to smile and then re-focus on what you are doing. Have a go at doing this, even when you are doing things like:

- Cooking
- Ironing
- Walking
- Listening to people talk
- Watching TV
- Listening to music
- Gardening
- Spending time with friends

 Playing with your children

By learning to live in the present, I want you to learn to become a 'human being' again, rather than a 'human doing'. Start enjoying the processes of the things you do. Every time you notice yourself living in the present and truly being absorbed in what you are doing, put a coin in your *Sort Your Life Out* jar. By now, your jar should be looking quite full.

Living in the present means being aware of what is happening right here, right now. It is everything you are experiencing in your doing, thinking and feeling. It means enjoying and being absorbed in the moment, and not letting your mind wander to other things around you, things that might happen in the future or things that happened in the past. When you live in this way, you will be better able to deal with whatever is going on in your life. By working through this programme, you will naturally find that by shutting up your internal dialogue more often and doing more of the things that make you feel good, you will automatically be present more of the time.

Smile, laugh and be happy

A smile is a curve that sets everything straight.
Shaggy Mumford

How many times a day do you think you smile and laugh? I know there are times when the last thing you want to do is smile, especially when you are stressed, worried, anxious or angry. But, did you know that simply moving your facial muscles into a smile (even a fake one) can make your emotional state change almost immediately?

Well, here are some facts about laughing and smiling that might motivate you to do more of both.

A friend of mine told me that he had read in a journal that children laugh an average of 500 times a day, but that by the time we become adults, we laugh only 15 times a day. What's more, a study by the School of Medicine at University of California at Irvine and the Loma Linda (CA) showed that people who watched a funny video for an hour experienced a drop in stress hormones that lasted between 12 and 24 hours. It's also been found that even anticipating something funny can help lower stress levels. So, what are you waiting for? Are you ready to give it a go, and see what happens?

Take a deep breath in and then, as you breathe out, allow your facial muscles to relax. Now, smile a big smile. It doesn't matter if it's a fake smile – you will start to feel different anyway. Try it again.

Now, do the opposite and pull the saddest face you can. Really frown and look downwards.

There is a big difference between these two extremes of emotional display – the 'happy' smile and the 'sad' face. Which one do you prefer?

I challenge you to make a conscious effort to smile over the next 21 days. I know that simply doing this will help you feel happier, and you will start to override any negative thoughts. You might even find that it's contagious and other people around you will start doing it, too.

Laughter is the shortest distance between two people.
Victor Borge

As for laughter, I want you to schedule in lots of things that make you laugh. Spend time with funny people, or watch or read something that cracks you up. You could even go one step further and even laugh for no reason at all. This is an activity that makes some people feel awkward, self-conscious or stupid, but the truth is that your body doesn't know the difference between real and fake laughter, so it produces happy chemicals in both cases. Apart from helping you feel happy, laughing and smiling can also help you feel more relaxed, which in turn boosts your immune system

At the end of each day, use your *Sort Your Life Out* journal to make a note of the times you remember laughing and smiling. The more you take notice of how you feel, the happier you will become. Smiling and laughing is a way of tricking your brain into thinking that everything's OK, even if it's not. By practising this, you will find yourself being happy for no reason at all.

That's just the way it is

Could it be that unhappiness is merely a state of mind, and that its solution also lies in our mind? Some people, such as positive psychologists (see page 194), believe that how we react to events in our life directly affects our happiness levels. So, let's have a look at how much you let things affect you.

Are there things that happen in your life that you allow to affect your mood when you don't need to? For example, how many times do you become unhappy, angry or upset when people are late? Or when they say something you don't much like? Or, indeed, when you have to do something you don't particularly want to do? Most of the things that we let affect us don't have to, but we simply choose to feel that way based on the countless times we have done that in the past. We tend not to see each situation from a fresh perspective; for example, just because you have got angry a number of times when your friend has been late to meet you, this does not mean you have to act that way every time in the future. If it hasn't made you feel great in the past, you can make the decision to try reacting in a different way. You may wait ten minutes and then leave and go home. Or you may decide to take a good book with you, and see each minute that he or she is late as bonus time to have a read. So many of our responses are automatic and also often negative; I suggest you question these habitual responses to make yourself feel better. And, as they say, 'don't sweat the small stuff'.

One of the things that makes the biggest difference to someone's happiness levels is how they react to things that they can't change. I want you to start recognizing when you are letting things that you can't control make you unhappy, stressed, sad, frustrated or anxious. For the next 21 days, I want you simply to let things be as they are and avoid overreacting, or even *reacting* to them. Say to yourself, or even out loud, *'That's just the way it is.'*

So, the next time you are stuck in a traffic jam, or someone tries to upset you, or you are late but can't do anything about it, rather than getting stressed or angry, say, 'That's just the way it is.' Then, smile and decide to react in a more productive way. Over the next 21 days, see how many times you can do this every day, and note how different it feels to choose to be happy. As with the other tools in this programme, you can motivate yourself and track your progress by topping up your *Sort Your Life Out* jar when you react in a more nourishing way.

 We may seek the world for happiness, but unless we carry it within us we will not find it.
Ralph Waldo Emerson

Some final suggestions ...

In addition to these *Sort Your Life Out* tools, there are some other general findings from the Happiness Equation research, which can help you identify areas of your life that may need some attention.

- *Try to regain a balance in your life:* Make sure you have enough time in your life dedicated to your family, your friends and yourself.

- *Invest in your close relationships:* Put some effort back into your close relationships. It's not important that you have lots of friends, but that you have close, trusting relationships.

- *Make the most of your holidays:* Use them to fulfil your interests and hobbies, challenge yourself to meet new people and break out of established patterns.

- *Exercise and rest:* Don't compromise, but make sure you have time for exercise and rest in your life, because you need both.

- *Set yourself a small challenge:* Remind yourself what it felt like to be stretched and have a clear purpose. This doesn't have to be anything major, like climbing Everest or setting up a charity – you can simply decide to do something that you would otherwise find it hard to complete. This may be something like learn to swim properly, tackle a great classic text that you've been putting off for ages, or try to cook something tricky like a soufflé.

Sort Your Life Out journal

DAY:

TOOLS I'M USING TODAY:

*

*

*

*

*

THOUGHTS, FEELINGS AND OBSERVATIONS:

*

*

*

*

*

3 POSITIVE THINGS THAT HAPPENED TODAY:

*

*

*

ANY OTHER NOTES E.G. FOOD/ACTIVITY DIARY:

SORT YOUR LIFE OUT:

Where Do I Go From Here?

Five short chapters on change

Chapter 1: I walk down a street and there's a deep hole in the pavement. I fall in. It takes forever to get out. It's my fault.

Chapter 2: I walk down the same street. I fall in the same hole again. It still takes a long time to get out. It's not my fault.

Chapter 3: I walk down the same street. I fall in the hole again. It's becoming a habit. It is my fault. I get out immediately.

Chapter 4: I walk down the same street and see the deep hole in the sidewalk. I walk around it.

Chapter 5: I walk down a different street.

Anonymous

This could be the story of your life. It could also be a summary of this book. You will be aware by now of the patterns you have been following up to now that have been making your life the way it is. However, what you now have, that you didn't when you started reading this book, is a different perspective and some tools to help you sort your life out.

There are many things you could be feeling at this stage of the programme. Some of you may be excited about how many changes you've made, and others may feel uncertain about what the future holds. It may be a good time for you to look back over your journal to acknowledge what you've done so far and this last chapter will help you look at how you are going to sustain your changes and continue to work on areas that still need your attention.

Where am I at?

This is a good time to go back to the *Sort Your Life Out* questionnaire (see pages 68–70). By filling it in (either in the book or online at http://www.sortyourlifeout.com/book) and comparing your scores before and after reading this book, and undertaking the tools, you will be able to see how well you've done, and which areas of your life have improved the most. As well as using this to track your progress, here are some thoughts that I'd like to leave you with as you start the rest of your journey ...

Why am I not perfect yet?

I don't assume, and neither should you, that just because

you've worked through this programme once, and done some things a few times, you'll carry on doing them forever. Equally, I know that just because you *know* something is the 'right' thing to do doesn't mean you'll carry on doing it. Most of us know what we have to do to sort our lives out, but that doesn't mean we actually go ahead and do it!

All change, no matter how minor, has to be maintained, and we have to learn how to do this. This is where the magic number 21 comes in. You really can change the way you are in your life by *practising* habits that will help you to become happier, healthier and more confident. And that means 21 times, or for 21 days.

As you now know, the key focus of this book is about practising doing things differently until you develop new habits. You can continue to use the tools, track them in your journal, and use your *Sort Your Life Out* jar for as long as you find them useful. Even if you have some time away from using them, you can always go back every now and then as a refresher. Everyone needs a little motivation from time to time. Re-acquainting yourself with the tools, or trying some you haven't attempted before, will soon help you to establish healthy, positive new habits that will help you make the changes you want to sort your life out for good.

A different view

One of the key points of this programme is the need to gain new ideas, perspectives and insights. By looking at things in a different way, you can work out what no longer serves a purpose in your life. With that knowledge, you can then let go of these things, beliefs and, sometimes even, people. For example, if you are training yourself to be more confident, you can reframe how you see a situation about which you feel a bit insecure. By seeing the possible outcomes in a realistic light, you may well realize that the worst-case scenario is not as bad as you had initially imagined. With that knowledge, you are one step closer to change, and with a little practice, you will establish the new habits that will bring and maintain your confidence.

The possibilities are endless

Just as many people don't realize how simple it can be to become fitter and healthier, I think that many people may also fail to realize how much happier they can be, and how much potential they have to achieve anything and everything they want.

What is your potential? Do you think there are limits to your possibilities or are they limitless? Recognizing the need to improve an area of our life, and anticipating the benefits it will bring, often unlocks the motivation to act and bring about change. And, encouragingly, the fact that we can do pretty much anything is backed up by the world of science. Years of research and observation make it clear that we only fully understand about 5 per cent of how our minds and bodies work. So we will never really know what we can achieve until we try.

By keeping track of your progress in your journal, you will start to see change unfolding, and, as it gathers pace, you will begin to see how much it is possible to change. When you

look back on your journal at a later date, you will know that
you can improve even more.

There is an old Chinese proverb that says a path with no
obstacles goes nowhere. There are always going to be difficulties, struggles and setbacks, because life is not supposed to
be easy. All that matters is how we deal with what comes up,
and stands in our way.

Be exceptional

Once you trust in the knowledge that anything is possible,
you can learn to apply yourself to achieve any goal. As I have
already pointed out, it's important to recognize your limitations and your imperfections. Nobody is perfect, and you
should never strive to be. But that should not stop you, me or
anyone from continually trying to improve. Many of us stop
striving for greatness because we associate success with perfection, and we feel that our own imperfections will limit us,
and limit what it is possible to achieve. But remember this:
being great or exceptional has nothing to do with perfection,
and everything to do with doing and being the best you can.

What are the qualities that exceptional people have?

- They love what they do and it's the doing of things
  they love
- They enjoy a challenge
- They bounce back and learn from setbacks
- They always feel they can do better
- They listen
- They are relentless
- They never give up and always follow through

What can we learn from that? The simple truth is that every one of these qualities is achievable, so making an effort to incorporate them into your daily life can make all the difference to how long it takes to get you where you want to go.

Believe in yourself

I know this is a cliché, but most people never realize their potential because they don't think they have any. The beliefs that you hold about yourself, in relation to your skills and abilities, and the environment in which you live, will determine how successful you will be. Our beliefs act as a framework for our behaviour – in other words, what we believe determines how we behave and what we get.

To change a habit, you will have to change your belief. This will require you to develop a new way of thinking. Just because you may have failed in the past, doesn't mean you will fail again. If you really want to change something in your life, know that by truly believing, it will happen, and you can find a way to make it so. Belief is the fuel of ambition. In attempting to do anything new or remotely ambitious in your life, you have to believe from the start that you can do it.

Take care of yourself

I think the biggest challenge in sorting your life out is making yourself a priority and taking better care of yourself. The degree to which you do this is dependent upon your desire for and attitude towards living a better life. To take care of yourself properly, you need to nourish yourself. Nourishment can take many different forms; it can include having a hobby, sleeping, eating well and surrounding yourself with supportive loving people. These are things that I hope you will have picked up all the way through this programme.

Any excuses you have for not looking after yourself (for example, your family, work or other commitments) should merely be viewed as being part of the challenge. Focusing on your difficulties is not going to help you change, nor is continuing to believe (just because you have been repeatedly told so) that doing what you want is going to be difficult. No matter what difficulties you face, or whatever your circumstances, taking care of yourself is really the only habit you need to have. One of the integral parts of taking care of yourself involves believing that you are worthy of care. Try not to be distracted from this very important job.

Being present

This book raises questions about the way we live our lives and how we perceive ourselves in the world in which we live. One of the key things that has cropped up in this book involves becoming a 'human being' again, rather than a 'human doing'. You can do this by being present. Unless you learn to live in the moment and let go of anxiety, fear, resentments and other distractions, they will rob you of your life. This is the reason why those who are very successful reach the top of their game; they live for every minute, they are there for every minute, and they enjoy every minute of what they do. Their being is in their doing, and that is what they focus on.

This is your life!

Have you ever heard the expression, 'Life is not a dress rehearsal'? No matter how many times I hear or say it, I never stop being amazed by how many people believe that there is nothing they can do to change their lives. I hope you now realize that you can change anything you want to change. And to cement that notion in your mind, I'd like you to work through the following exercise:

Being 99

- Imagine you are 99 years old, and you're looking back over your life. What would you wish you had done *less* of? Write down two or three things in your *Sort Your Life Out* journal. Examples could include being critical, worrying, working too hard, or procrastinating.
- Now, what would you wish you had done *more* of? Write down some of these things in your journal, too. Examples might be relaxing, travelling to new places, spending time with family and friends, or laughing and having fun.

Well, here comes the great news ... chances are that you're not 99 years old yet, so if you had any regrets when you were doing this exercise, you can start to take steps now to make sure they don't become reality.

Look at the list of things you wish you'd done more of. If these are things you really want to do, make time to do them. Then look at the list of things you wish you'd done less of. What's stopping you from changing them? Again, it's not too late to stop doing these things. You can decide to do whatever you want in a different way.

By making a personal commitment to our own individual transformational process, we automatically begin to transform the world around us.
Shakti Gawain

Get support

We live in a society where we're expected to cope with all of life's pressures, and yet, so many of us believe that asking for help is a sign of weakness. Well, guess what? That's nonsense!

You are a human being and so there will always be times when you may find life a little challenging. This doesn't make you weak, it makes you just like everyone else. So you can either decide to do everything alone and risk struggling, or you can get some support and encouragement.

It may be that you enlist the help of people with whom you live, or your colleagues, a close friend, a partner or someone else who you feel understands you. You may even get support from more than one person. I suggest you tell them what you want to achieve and how you're planning to do it. You never know, they might even feel inspired to join you. By sharing your aims, you'll also be making a stronger commitment to your goal, and providing yourself with support when you need a helping hand. Remember that we all need people to support us in what we do, and that support can make a big difference.

What else is there?

There is a lot of material in this book, and it has been written in such a way that you can revisit any section of the programme whenever you want. However, I would like to continue helping you sort your life out, so if you are interested in receiving my free 'Pete Cohen Keep Going' emails, visit the Sort Your Life Out website at http://www.sortyourlifeout. com/book, and sign up. All you have to do is enter your email address.

You can also let us know how you get on and what's working for you by emailing us at info@sortyourlifeout.com. This helps us get an idea of how we can keep making the programme better, and it's always lovely to hear your success stories. The Sort Your Life Out website also has lots of other information that may interest you. You can, for example, fill in the Happiness Equation and get your happiness score. You can also download the free Relaxation and Transformation mp3 track that is a part of my weight-loss programme.

For those of you who are interested in losing weight and getting fit, then check out my weight-loss programme, at http://www.petecohen.tv. This is a fantastic opportunity for me to coach you personally over 21 days. The programme has already helped thousands of people and it can help you, too. You can take a free trial by going to the site, to find out how it all works, and how it has helped other people. And if you decide you want to sign up, you can get a 50 per cent discount. The programme retails at £59.99, but if you enter the promo word SYLO, you will get it for £29.99. It's too good an opportunity to pass over...

It's up to you...

As you know by now, I encourage you to see the process of sorting your life out as a way of choosing the way you play the game of life. You get to pick your own rules, make choices that are right for you, and set your own attitude. This book is simply a guide, because ultimately you choose how to live your life. All I really want is that you feel great and enjoy yourself on the ride.

Just before I finish, I want to share a poem with you, called 'Lessons from an Oyster'.

There once was an oyster whose story I tell, who found that some sand had got in his shell.
It was only a grain, but it gave him great pain. For oysters have feelings although they're so plain.
Now, did he berate the harsh workings of fate that had brought him to such a deplorable state?
Did he curse at the government, cry for election, and claim that the sea should have given him protection?
'No,' he said to himself as he lay on a shell, 'since I cannot remove it, I shall try to improve it.'
Now the years have rolled around, as the years always do, and he came to his ultimate destiny – stew.
And the small grain of sand that had bothered him so was a beautiful pearl, all richly aglow.

Good luck, and I wish you every success in sorting your life out.

Pete

Endnotes

1 'The Brain Plasticity Revolution: the Brain that Changes Itself', Mottram, C., and Rymer, W.Z. (2008), *Neurology Today*, 8 (11), p. 16.

2 'Components of Attention', Posner, M.I., and Boies, S.J. (1971), *Psychological Review*, 78, pp. 296–408.

3 'Positive Psychology Progress: Empirical Validation of Interventions', Seligman, M.E.P., Steen, T.A., Park, N., and Peterson, C. (2005), *American Psychologist*, 60 (5), pp. 410–421.

4 Is Well-Being U-Shaped over the Life Cycle?, Oswald, A. and Blanchflower, D. (2008), *Social Science & Medicine*, 66 (6), pp. 1,733–1,749.

5 Norwich Union commissioned research with Redshift Research Ltd amongst 1,511 UK adults in May 2008.

6 *Satisfaction: The science of finding true fulfilment*, Dr G. Berns, Henry Holt & Co, 2005.

7 'Health, Wealth and Happiness', Smith, D.M., Langa, K.M., Kabeto, M.U., and Ubel, P.A. (2005), *Psychological Science*, 16 (9) pp. 663–666.

Further Resources

If you are looking for some more resources to help you enjoy your life more, then check out my *Sort Your Life Out* Box. It's full of proven tools and resources that will provide you with even more everyday practical solutions to help you achieve long-lasting change in your life.

The box contains:

- A 5-DVD set of my incredible *Sort Your Life Out* Live Event in London, 2008
- My step-by-step *Habit-Busting Workbook*, giving you the tools you need to break any unwanted habit and create healthy new ones
- My step-by-step *Fear-Busting Workbook*, empowering you to stop procrastinating and beat any fear that is holding you back
- My step-by-step *Life DIY Workbook*, giving you more practical ways to create the life you want
- A music CD, created specifically to help relax your mind and body
- A *Sort Your Life Out* journal, for you to record and monitor your progress
- A 4-CD set of my inspiring *Sort Your Life Out* Slimming audio CDs

To purchase the box and find out more visit, http://www.sortyourlifeout.com/book.

Index

Sort Your Life Out journal

DAY:

TOOLS I'M USING TODAY:

*
*
*
*
*

THOUGHTS, FEELINGS AND OBSERVATIONS:

*
*
*
*
*

3 POSITIVE THINGS THAT HAPPENED TODAY:

*
*
*

ANY OTHER NOTES E.G. FOOD/ACTIVITY DIARY:

Sort Your Life Out journal

DAY:

TOOLS I'M USING TODAY:

*

*

*

*

*

THOUGHTS, FEELINGS AND OBSERVATIONS:

*

*

*

*

*

3 POSITIVE THINGS THAT HAPPENED TODAY:

*

*

*

ANY OTHER NOTES E.G. FOOD/ACTIVITY DIARY:

DAY:

TOOLS I'M USING TODAY:

-
-
-
-
-

THOUGHTS, FEELINGS AND OBSERVATIONS:

-
-
-
-
-

3 POSITIVE THINGS THAT HAPPENED TODAY:

-
-
-

ANY OTHER NOTES E.G. FOOD/ACTIVITY DIARY:

DAY:

TOOLS I'M USING TODAY:

*

*

*

*

*

THOUGHTS, FEELINGS AND OBSERVATIONS:

*

*

*

*

*

3 POSITIVE THINGS THAT HAPPENED TODAY:

*

*

*

ANY OTHER NOTES E.G. FOOD/ACTIVITY DIARY: